MOUSEMAN

The Legacy of Robert Thompson of Kilburn

by Patricia Lennon & David Joy

Great Northern Books
PO Box 213, Ilkley, LS29 9WS
www.greatnorthernbooks.co.uk

The expressions "Mouseman", "Robert Thompson's"
and "Robert Thompson's Craftsmen Ltd, and the
three-dimensional carved mouse, are registered
trademarks.

ISBN: 978-1-905080-38-0

Design and cover photography: Mark Pickthall
Layout: David Burrill

Printed in Germany

CIP Data
A catalogue for this book is available from the British
Library

Photographs from Robert Thompson's Craftsmen
Ltd, Yorkshire Post Newspapers, National Trust
Photographic Library, David Joy and the Star Inn.
Harome.

Royalties from the sales of this book are being
donated by Robert Thompson's Craftsmen Ltd to a
British tree planting scheme.

CONTENTS

PART TWO – ON THE TRAIL OF THE MOUSE

Seven circular and scenic driving tours in North Yorkshire and Cumbria – plus a walking tour of York – taking in locations of 'mouse' work as well as other places of interest.

Note: Many of the places included in these tours of the Mouseman's work are places of worship and are only open to the public at certain times. To avoid any disappointment, it is always advisable to phone ahead and check opening times.

FOREWORD

by Alan Titchmarsh

(Yorkshire Post)

I first noticed 'the mouse' on the leg of a small table in the side chapel of Otley Parish Church, where I was a choirboy in the 1950s. Then I found one carved into the oak organ casing just above my head. I learned about Robert Thompson, gradually, and on Sunday afternoons my dad would take us up the Dales in the back of his Mini van – one such trip was to Kilburn and I was amazed by the stacks of oak planking.

Many years later, when I got married, I discovered that our bridesmaids' brothers had been to Ampleforth, and that the huge refectory tables in their south-west London dining room – and the chairs – all had mice on them. We decided to save up. It took us seven years, but finally we were able to buy a new 'kitchen' table and ten chairs. We dine at the table and sit in the chairs every day of our lives and have never regretted the saving up!

The craftsmanship of Robert Thompson and his craftsmen, and the tactile qualities of the furniture, are things I will always treasure – along with the 'Mouseman' tray off which I eat my TV suppers!

INTRODUCTION

by Ian Thompson Cartwright

As a small child, I would spend many hours in the workshop, making simple wooden boats to sail down the beck that runs through the village of Kilburn. I would listen to the craftsmen who had been trained by my Great Grandfather, Robert Thompson, talking about the outstanding jobs that they had worked on over the years. The pride I saw on their faces is repeated today when one of our craftsmen turns, stands back and views the item of furniture that he has just completed.

By following the tours listed within this book, you will be able to visit some of the sites where furniture produced by Great Grandfather and his craftsmen still stands as magnificently as the day it was installed.

I like to imagine those craftsmen admiring their own skill and also, perhaps, a little surprised in realising just what they had created from a working drawing produced by their master, 'The Mouseman of Kilburn'.

Even today, I still experience a tremendous feeling of pride and joy when, visiting establishments such as Ampleforth College and York Minster, I discover an item of furniture that was made by my forefathers that I did not know was in existence.

The location of many of the churches and the countryside that you will pass through when following the 'Trail of the Mouse' really does show the North of England at its best. I personally have spent many a summer evening after a day in the workshop, driving along the country lanes, passing through the idyllic villages and admiring the views across the moors when covered in that beautiful purple heather carpet.

Should you be a 'mouse' collector or someone with an interest in Thompson furniture, I am certain you will enjoy viewing many of the previously unpublished family photographs that will provide you with an insight into the life and work of a very remarkable man, 'The Mouseman of Kilburn'.

Opposite:
Back Row Left to Right: Simon Thompson Cartwright and Giles Thompson Cartwright Front Row Left to Right: Ian Thompson Cartwright and Peter Thompson Cartwright.

1 ROBERT THOMPSON – EARLY YEARS AND INFLUENCES

Handle a piece of Thompson furniture today and you are immediately in touch with the past. Each piece comprises layers of English history: the style and design will reflect the vision of a man born in the nineteenth century whose original inspiration came from ecclesiastical craftsmen of the Middle Ages. The history contained within that simple piece of furniture will unfold in this book - the story of Robert Thompson, the Mouseman of Kilburn.

It was a simple appreciation of craftsmanship and the natural beauties of English oak that inspired a young, country carpenter, at the start of the twentieth century, to turn his back on the new innovations of mass production and instead rekindle the traditional wood carving techniques of a former age. Today, thousands of people across the world, inspired by the furniture he created, share the same appreciation of natural beauty and traditional skills. This is Robert Thompson's legacy.

The story starts in Kilburn, a picturesque village nestling in the Hambleton Hills, to the north of York. The village today is little different from the place where Robert Thompson was born in 1876 and where he lived for most of his life. The son of a local joiner, Robert Thompson was brought up in a small Elizabethan cottage in the centre of the village. The cottage eventually became his own home and today it remains the centre for the company he founded. Young Robert attended the local village school where he gained a good grounding in basic academic skills. At the age of 15, his father decided that Robert should learn a trade and, against the boy's wishes, arranged for him to serve an engineering apprenticeship with the Garnett Wire Company in Cleckheaton, a busy town right at the smoking heart of West Yorkshire's industrial belt.

Robert later recorded his dismay at this drastic change of environment and described his years of apprenticeship as 'five years of penal servitude'. At the age of twenty, he persuaded his father to allow him to return to Kilburn and work with him in his joinery business. But the years in Cleckheaton were not entirely fruitless. During his apprenticeship, Robert's travels between home and his place of work took him through the city of Ripon with its imposing cathedral. Here he marvelled at the craftsmanship of the cathedral's mediaeval woodcarvings particularly those of the master carver, William Bromflet. In later life, he spoke of this early experience as his inspiration to 'bring back to life the spirit of mediaeval oak work, which had been dead for so many long years'.

Back in Kilburn, as a young carpenter in his father's business, Robert Thompson's days were spent in mundane but essential repairs and construction of farm buildings. But the inspiration of Bromflet remained. Ideas and passion were slowly but very definitely being forged in the young man's heart and mind.

At the end of the nineteenth century, the work of a country tradesman was hard and the hours were long. However, Robert Thompson's drive was so great that what little free time he had from mending fences and building barns, he dedicated to learning more about the ancient craft of the mediaeval wood carvers: both the materials they used and the tools with which they worked. This early research led directly to the formation of his unique style of furniture - English oak worked with an adze to produce a distinctive ripple surface effect. This combination of hard wearing, beautifully grained wood complemented by the unusual adzed finish, was to become his signature, making his work easily identifiable with or without the presence of the later 'trademark' mouse.

During these formative years, whilst continuing his everyday trade as a country joiner, Robert also began to lay down supplies of oak for natural seasoning. Just as there were easier materials to work with than tough English oak, and contemporary tools were easier to handle than the mediaeval adze, so too, kiln drying offered a speedier means of seasoning wood prior to carving. Robert Thompson, perfectionist that he was, would have none of it. He believed that only natural seasoning could produce wood that would retain its beauty for decades even centuries. Thompson's approach was to saw whole trees lengthways into long planks, in the early years with handsaws and later by machine. These were then stacked into piles, each plank separated by a small stick (a latt) and allowed to dry in the open air for up to five years.

It may appear that Robert Thompson's approach to his craft was almost perverse in adopting materials and techniques to make the task as laborious as possible. But it should be remembered that, to him, mass production was anathema: what truly mattered was to create a work of true craftsmanship that would stand the test of time. Apprentices recalled that he often encouraged them towards excellence by reminding them that their work would still be in use in three hundred years' time. And his 'obsession' has been vindicated. Today, the company he founded continues to produce furniture, in English oak, seasoned in the same way, and using the same ancient tools and techniques that he revived - and the order book is full for many months ahead.

However, back in Kilburn, at the dawn of the twentieth century, Robert Thompson, then in his mid twenties, could not possibly have realised how successful his vision would turn out to be. There remained the day-to-day necessity of earning a living, added to which was the cost of investing in oak for seasoning. To augment his carpentry work, he turned to stone masonry and several of his early gargoyles and First World War memorials exist in the villages around Kilburn. During the pre-First World War period, he also undertook his first ecclesiastical work - a pulpit for Yearsley church and altar rails for Harome.

The outbreak of the First World War brought turmoil and change to Kilburn as to all villages, towns and cities across the country. As the breadwinner of the family and a provider of local jobs and services, Robert Thompson was exempt from active duty. However, his workforce

Opposite:
Top:
A finished church screen is proudly displayed by Robert (far right) amd his craftsmen.

Bottom:
Robert at work in his studio.

Robert and his only daughter, Elsie, in 1909 with one of his first ecclesiastical commissions — a pulpit for Yearsley Parish Church.

Opposite: Fine clothes for the country craftsman on his wedding day in 1905. The local newspaper described his bride, Ada, as 'attired in a dress of grey silk trimmed with chiffon and chiffon hat to match; she carried a bouquet composed of lilies of the valley and maiden hair fern'. The couple were reported to have taken their honeymoon in Goole.

was dramatically reduced with many of his younger staff posted overseas as part of the war effort.

With the end of the human turmoil of the Great War, millions of people welcomed a return to the 'ordinary' lives they had known before 1914. But for Robert Thompson, events were about to take him on a very different track from that of the village carpenter. His ambition to rekindle 'the spirit of mediaeval oak work' was about to become reality.

Looking slightly uncomfortable in a studio portrait with Elsie.

Opposite: Robert in his office, wearing the white coat he invariably donned when drawing. Resting on the massive table are his reference books, which are still in use today.

Robert Thompson Cartwright and John Cartwright, grandsons of Robert Thompson.

A few words with his first great grandchild, Jane Cartwright.

Robert outside the drawing office in his favourite three-piece suit.

Pipe smokers discuss the topic of the day. It is thought that the gentleman with the trilby is Mr Jowett, from whom Robert bought a Jowett car, and that the other figure is his chauffeur. In the background is Robert's cottage and his beloved rose garden.

TO THE MEMORY
OF
THOMAS LORD
BORN AT THIRSK NOVEMBER 23rd 1755

HE ESTABLISHED THE FIRST GROUND KNOWN AS LORDS, THE
HOME OF THE M.C.C. IN DORSET SQUARE ST. MARYLEBONE
IN 1787 SUBSEQUENTLY REMOVING ITS TURF TO A SECOND
SITE AT NORTH BANK REGENTS PARK IN 1811 AND FINALLY
TO ST. JOHN'S WOOD IN 1814

THIS TABLET WAS PRESENTED IN HIS HONOUR TO THE
THIRSK CRICKET CLUB BY THE COMMITTEE AND MEMBERS
OF THE M.C.C. TO MARK THE BICENTENARY OF HIS BIRTH

THOMAS LORD

1755   BI-CENTENARY   1955

Invitation to attend a luncheon in July 1955 marking the bi-centenary of Thirsk-born Thomas Lord, who established Lord's cricket ground. The commemorative plaque was made by Robert Thompson, who in the photograph is seen sitting as he attends one of his last public engagements.

Opposite: On the step of what is now known as Mouseman Cottage. On fine days Robert regularly sat here to read his morning paper, the Yorkshire Post. A true countryman, he was a great lover of dogs and used the spaniel when he went rabbiting around the White Horse.

2 THE HOUSE OF THE MOUSE

Opposite:
Left:
Father Paul
Nevill, Robert
Thompson's
first major
patron.
(courtesy
Ampleforth
Abbey School)

Right:
The crucifix at
Ampleforth,
completed in
1919 and the
start of a
lifelong
association
between
Robert
Thompson and
Ampleforth
College.

Bottom:
A page from
Robert
Thompson's
ledger for
1936, showing
the diverse
range of pieces
produced for
Ampleforth
College and
the prices
charged.

The turning point in Robert Thompson's career was a fortuitous meeting with Father Paul Nevill, a Catholic Priest from Ampleforth College. In conversation with one of his parishioners, Sydney Mawe, Father Paul outlined his plans to erect a large crucifix in the cemetery at Ampleforth but explained that he was having difficulty in locating a carpenter with a piece of oak large enough to carry out the project. Sydney Mawe introduced him to his neighbour Robert Thompson and the contract was confirmed.

That was the start of a long-lasting friendship between both men and a working relationship between the College and Robert Thompson's company that remains alive today. And yet, were it not for the craftsman's optimism and pragmatism, that opportunity may have been missed, as he revealed later in life:

`I said "Yes" to Father Paul without hesitation knowing I hadn't the oak and I didn't know where it was coming from but I wasn't going to say "no"'.

It was also around this time that Thompson introduced his famous trademark: a mouse carved in relief into every piece of work. No one knows exactly when or where he carved his first mouse but an extract from a letter in 1949 to the Reverend John Fisher allows Robert Thompson to explain its creation in his own words:

'The origin of the mouse as my mark was almost in the way of being an accident. I and another carver were carving a huge cornice for a screen and he happened to say something about being as poor as a church mouse. I said I'll carve a mouse here and did so, then it struck me what a lovely trade mark. This is about 30 years ago'.

Later to his grandsons, who continued his work, he explained how he was humoured by the thought of a mouse scraping and chewing its way through the hardest wood, working away quietly while nobody takes any notice. He saw an immediate parallel with his own workshop, hidden away in the Hambleton Hills and so also was born his motto, 'industry in quiet places'.

The mouse, created as a whimsy, has become a lasting and distinctive trademark - probably one of the earliest 'logos' created in the 20th century to still be around, unchanged, today. However, Robert Thompson never let the distinctive little symbol dominate his work. It is usually tucked away in unobtrusive corners, providing a special challenge to those who seek it out in dimly lit church interiors.

From that first commission at Ampleforth, Robert Thompson's reputation rapidly spread. Over the next thirty five years, the Thompson mouse was to find a wide range of homes across the British Isles and farther afield, from small country churches to Westminster Abbey; academic institutions to town halls; corporate headquarters to country hotels; and in the private homes of individuals who appreciated the quality and craftsmanship that Robert Thompson and his workers brought to

93

Ampleforth College account (Rev. E. Fitzsimons)

il	6	To alteration to buffet cleaning etc.	2 5 -		
	14	" 150 chairs @ 30/- each	225 - -		
		" 16 tables @ £16. each	256 - -		
		" two special octagonal tables @ £23.ea	46 - -		
		" 12 chairs @ £3. each	36 - -		
		" one serving table	6 - -		
		" two easy chairs with cushions	20 - -		
4.	8	" 15 masters desks @ £9. each	135 - -	210
		" 35 low back chairs @ 30/- ea.	52 10 -	
		" two special inlaid burr tables @ 75/-	7 10 -	796 5
	10	By cheque £481. on a/c		
	2	" £4. 8s.	485 8
		Nett balance due	310 17
	21	By allowance	7 10

The famous 'mouse'. In Robert Thompson's day an apprentice was not considered to be qualified until he could carve the mouse to his master's satisfaction.

Opposite: This staircase completed by Robert Thompson in 1924 for Upsall Castle, near Thirsk, is 'pre-mouse'. It is said that Robert offered at a later date to 'sign' the work by adding his famous mouse but the owner declined, arguing that a piece without the tell-tale trademark would have greater rarity value. The staircase has recently been restored following water damage caused by a leaking roof.

every piece.

As commissions started to increase, so too did the number of craftsmen and apprentices at the tiny workshop in Kilburn, reaching a total workforce of about 35 men and boys at the time of Robert Thompson's death.

While the mouse travelled far and wide, its creator, Robert Thompson, stayed firmly rooted in his home village of Kilburn. He married a local girl, lived and worked in the same cottage where he had spent his childhood and where he, in turn, brought up his only child, Elsie.

One visitor to his office commented: 'I recall a well-dressed man with a military type moustache. The fire was on and he had two Labradors with him.'

In 1955 he died and was buried in the small church graveyard in Kilburn where a simple tombstone marks his grave. His real and lasting monument is just a stone's throw away at the House of the Mouse - the workshop he founded and which today continues the traditional skills of wood carving that he revived and made his own.

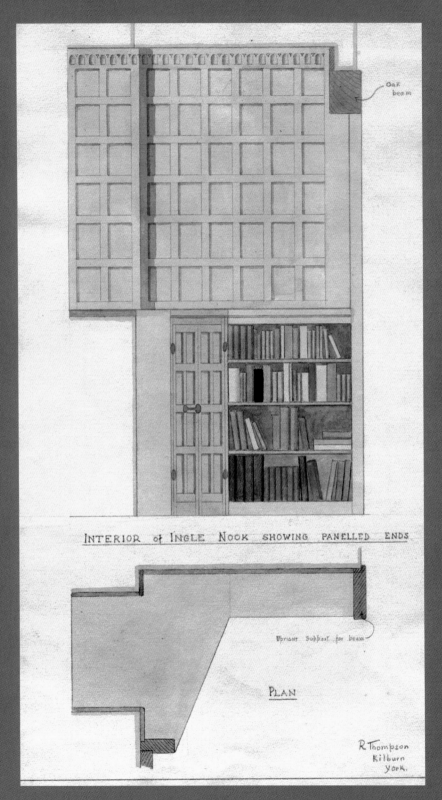

Oak beam

INTERIOR of INGLE NOOK SHOWING PANELLED ENDS

Upright support for beam

PLAN

R Thompson
Kilburn
York.

Many of Robert Thompson's working drawings are objects of beauty in their own right. This design for the interior of an ingle nook dates from the late 1920s or early '30s.

Opposite: Robert is the left-hand figure in this group of craftsmen outside a country house.

The Kilburn workshop, about 1925.

The Bedford lorry that was long used to deliver furniture made at Kilburn. Robert Thompson is stood on the lorry as what looks like a very heavy refectory table is heaved on board.

Opposite: The radiator cap on the lorry was quite properly made of wood with a 'mouse' on top.

Kilburn in 1959 or 1960, showing Thompson's mock Tudor workshop and behind it the new drying shed that has just been erected. Mouseman Cottage on the left of the entrance is still partially thatched. On its right is the old engine house, where a steam engine was once kept to drive machinery in the workshop. When Robert Thompson was young it housed a cow, which he had to take out to graze on the common ground before he set off for school. Note the timber stacked in the foreground and the United bus timetable on the wall opposite.

Opposite:
John Cartwright, Robert Thompson's grandson, carving in the old workshop in June 1953. A fascinating array of tools is on view.

This drawing of a mouse, chisel, mallet and plane dates from 1945 and is thought to have been given to Robert as a thank you by someone with artistic flair.

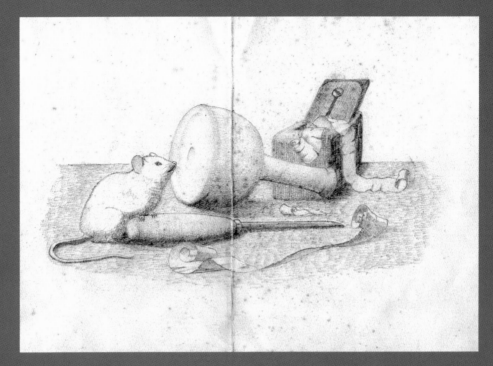

Opposite:
The living room of Mouseman Cottage. The fireplace, which features early 'mice' and a carved frieze, is still there today. The very early Thompson chair with leatherwork and turned legs is a copy of a 16th or 17th century piece. This chair is shown at top left in the drawing of three chairs on page 47.

Kilburn church, with Robert Thompson's final resting place in the foreground. The company's workshop is seen behind the church.

3 THE MOUSEMAN LEGACY LIVES ON – KILBURN TODAY

Opposite:
Top:
Despite often carrying the most minimal of addresses, letters find their way to Robert Thompson's from all parts of the world.

Bottom:
Stacks of oak outside the Mouseman Visitor Centre in Kilburn.

Visitors to Kilburn today will find it little changed in appearance from Robert Thompson's time: a huddle of cottages, either side of a brook, define the main street. The whole scene conforms to the image of a typical sleepy English village. It is the kind of place in which the casual visitor may imagine nothing much happens. And yet from here items of furniture are despatched to the far most corners of the globe. Indeed aficionados of Thompson's work travel from across the world to visit his birthplace. Their travels are rewarded as the village and its surrounding countryside offer much for 'mouse' enthusiasts.

The Mouseman Visitor Centre presents a fascinating history of Robert Thompson, and includes replicas of the interiors of his cottage and workshop, complete with original examples of furniture carved by the master himself. Also included are exquisite hand coloured designs for furniture and room settings. Equally fascinating are the order books and ledgers on display which record early customers' requirements and the prices paid - chairs at 30 shillings each and tables at £16 represented a sound investment for Ampleforth College in 1936.

The Visitor Centre is also a focus for living history as visitors may observe craftsmen at work, demonstrating the type of tools, techniques and skills that Robert Thompson practised. The craftsmen are happy to provide a commentary as they work, explaining the origins of a particular design or the technique being used. Visitors may also be able to try their hand at adzing and will quickly appreciate the skill required.

Directly opposite the Visitor Centre are the current show rooms and workshops. The range of domestic furniture produced in the Kilburn workshop today includes many pieces that remain true to Robert Thompson's original designs. As in the earliest days of the company, ecclesiastical work and civic commissions are an important element of the business. In fact, the links with Robert Thompson's original work are never far away: original books on mediaeval carvings, which provided inspiration for Robert Thompson, are still used today for reference in new commissioned pieces.

On receiving a new commission, the designer will research where the piece is to be placed and formulate designs for the client's approval. A working drawing will then be produced along with a cutting list, which will stipulate the amount and type of timber required. If the piece is to become part of a standard range of furniture, a prototype will then be produced. Once full approval has been given to the design, it is then passed onto one of the company's thirty or so craftsmen who will bring the piece to life.

Not only the designs but also the actual production processes are little changed from Robert Thompson's days. At the company's workshop, a special viewing gallery allows visitors to observe the craftsman at work on the actual production of pieces of

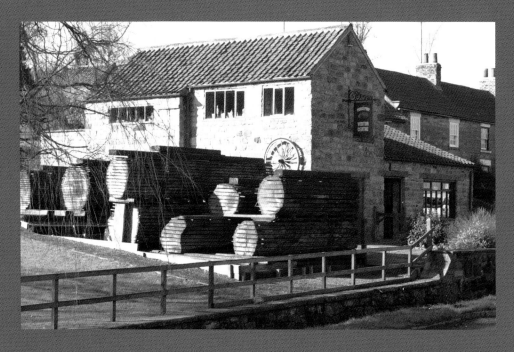

The workshop at Kilburn has been featured on many TV programmes. The BBC's Antiques Roadshow, pictured during filming, confirmed the collectable status of Thompson furniture –– the antiques of tomorrow.

furniture.

The starting point for any piece of Thompson furniture will typically begin in a field or forest, many years before the actual carving process begins. The company sources oak from across the country, preferring wood that has grown in the north of England and purchasing between two hundred and three hundred felled oak trees every year. Much of the timber comes from managed estates that are certified by the Forestry Stewardship Council, an international organisation founded in 1992 that seeks to ensure long-term timber supplies at the same time as protecting the environment.

In 2006, Ian Thompson Cartwright was invited to the Hirsel Estate, near Coldstream, home of the late Sir Alec Douglas-Hume, to inspect some 200-year-old oaks that had just been felled. Their massive dimensions made them ideally suited for the creation of table tops and sideboards, so they were purchased and taken to Robert Thompson's sawmill at Ampleforth to be converted from the round into planks. They will now be stacked and seasoned naturally for several years before the process of hand carving, fuming and waxing can begin.

Visitors to Kilburn will see huge stacks of sawn English oak, being stored and seasoned in the open air, in the traditional way. At any one time there is more than five years' worth of oak in storage.

Each tree is personally inspected before purchase and the age of the tree is calculated. Damage to a tree suffered many years previously from frost or pest, can show up as 'ring shake' or 'star shake', which detract from the appearance of the grain. Lightning strikes will result in the timber not taking colour during the fuming process. As Thompson furniture is not stained or painted, it is impossible to hide such defects in the finished piece of furniture.

Each piece of Thompson furniture is taken from start to finish by one craftsman. All the craftsmen - and they range in age from twenty-year-olds to septuagenarians - joined the company from school and have been trained in-house. They serve a four or five year apprenticeship, working under different carvers so that they experience a range of approaches and styles. This ensures that each craftsman finds scope for the expression of his own personal style within the overall guidelines of the Thompson approach.

The in-house training and apprenticeship system leads to smooth transfer of skills and maintains a direct line from today's craftsmen back to Robert Thompson himself.

When starting a particular job, whether a piece from the current range or a specially commissioned piece, the craftsman responsible will personally select the timber. He will look for specific qualities of grain or colour that will enhance the design in question and also ensure that the timber selected has been seasoned correctly. Wood for a tabletop, which will typically be two inches thick, will have been seasoned outside for a minimum of four years.

Having selected the appropriate timber, the craftsman will then carry out rough cutting to shape. The piece proceeds to the bench, where the actual carving and assembling will take place. The length of time spent at this stage will depend on the piece in question: typically, a dining chair will take twenty hours of bench time; a bureau may take four weeks.

Opposite:
Top:
A prized feature of the museum, which forms part of the visitor centre, is Robert Thompson's exquisite copy of Sudbury's Hutch, acquired after being bought back at a sale in Pickering. The original was given to Louth parish church in Lincolnshire circa 1495 by a vicar named Sudbury. The doors are carved with profile portraits of Henry VII and his consort Elizabeth of York, while the central panel has the badges of Lancaster and York below a crown.

Massive oak trees on the Hirsel Estate that were felled in 2006 and then converted into planks. They have now been stacked and will season naturally until 2012, when they will be transformed into beautiful pieces of furniture.

Sawn oak logs being delivered to the workshop – a familiar sight in Kilburn village.

Craftsmen at work can be seen
from the viewing gallery in the
workshop. The inset shows an adze
being skilfully used to create the
familiar ripple-effect surface by
carving scallops of oak.

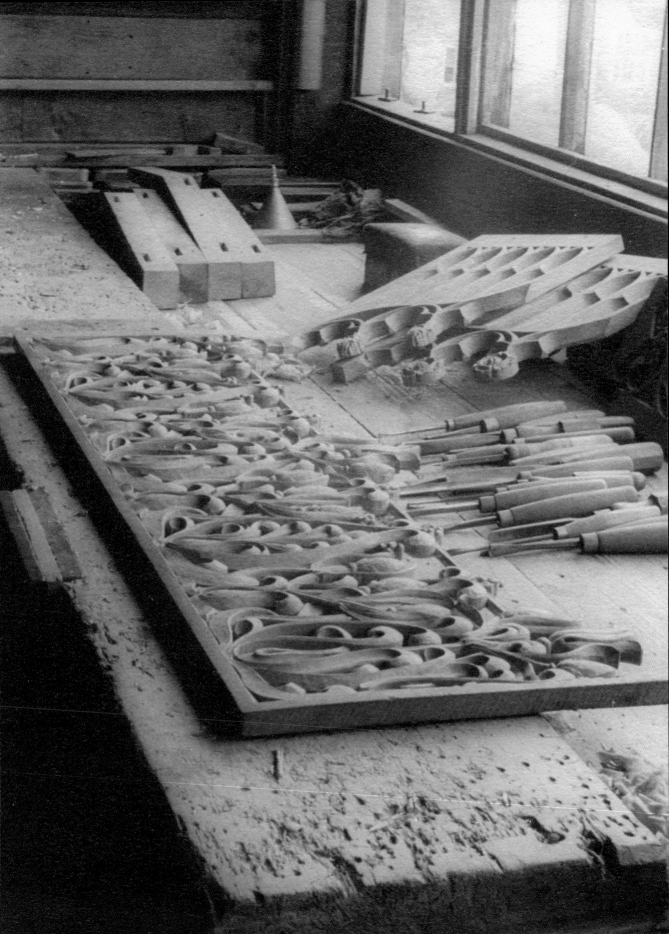

It is at this stage that the adzing process takes place, which gives the surface of Thompson furniture its distinctive rippled appearance. The craftsman first marks out in pencil the lines that the adze will follow, matching the direction of the grain on the surface of the wood. The piece of timber is placed on the floor and the craftsman stands on top of it. With a gentle pendulum motion, he swings the adze slowly between his legs, slicing slivers of wood from the surface. Seeing the adze used in this way, alongside heavy boots and hard hands, to produce a soft rippled surface, demonstrates the supreme skill of the master. After adzing, the wood is sanded by hand and then placed in the fuming chamber, which is filled with ammonia vapour. The alkali in the ammonia reacts with the acid in the oak to impart a soft honey colour on the surface of the oak. This method of colouring oak was used in the Middle Ages, using urine instead of ammonia. The fuming process was employed by Robert Thompson in preference to the staining and dying processes, more prevalent in the early nineteenth century.

Generally taking 24 hours, the fuming time can be varied according to a customer's preference for a particular hue. The eventual results are affected by various factors including the age and condition of the wood and even the outside weather. Once again, the idiosyncratic nature of the process ensures that each piece of Mouseman furniture is unique.

Once the fuming process is complete, the craftsman will apply a wax paste by brush to the surface of the wood, which is then polished by hand. If the surface is likely to be exposed to moisture, a polyurethane varnish is used.

The actual assembly of a piece of furniture also follows a centuries old tradition. All mortise and tenon joints are doweled for strength and stability using oak dowels, which each craftsman makes himself as part of the whole production process.

The final stage in the production process is the upholstery. Chair seats are webbed with cotton and finished with leather from a Scottish-based company. The leather comes from Highland cattle as a byproduct of the meat industry.

On leaving the Mouseman Visitor Centre and showroom, 'mouse' enthusiasts may be interested to visit St Mary's church in Kilburn. Here they will find early examples of Thompson's work and that of his successors, including an unusual set of oak headstones in the graveyard. Inside the church are a 'breeches' bible showcase, a litany desk, lectern and traceried pulpit, all bearing the discreet but distinctive mouse trademark. Note also on the lectern a carved lizard indicating this as a piece designed by the Architect Ernest Walker, whose family crest featured a lizard. Similar 'mouse' and 'lizard' work can be found in St Luke's Church in York. In 1958, the chapel of St Thomas at Kilburn was refurbished as a memorial to Robert Thompson, the company's craftsmen producing all the chapel's furnishing in the distinctive adzed style. To sit within the cool, stillness of this ancient chapel, surrounded by beautiful hand crafted oak, allows the visitor to contemplate, and perhaps share, the quiet passion that motivated Robert Thompson.

Whilst in Kilburn, visitors can combine their quest for the mouse

Opposite: Tools set out for some intricate carving in the workshop. In the background are sharpening stones along with an oil can that are now in the museum.

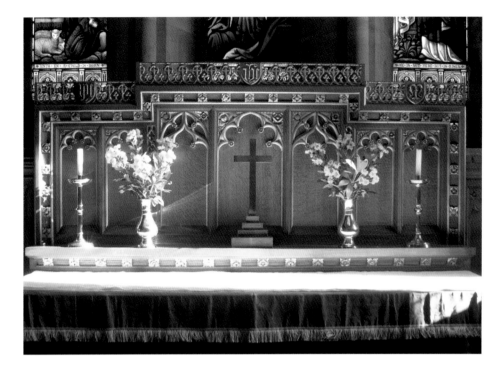

Altar inside Kilburn church.

Opposite: Design for a filing cabinet. The butterfly hinges date the cabinet to an earlier period before Robert Thompson moved over to the more characteristic round hinges.

with a search for refreshment at the Forresters Arms. Not surprisingly, being situated next to Thompson's workshop, this delightful village inn is overrun with 'mice' of the wooden variety.

Design for Filing Cabinet.

In English Oak. with moveable shelves.

4

HOW TO DATE MOUSEMAN FURNITURE
Ian Cartwright

The mouse trademark first appeared on various items of furniture produced by Robert Thompson back in the early 1920s. Mice were carved with raised heads and front legs. The style was modified shortly after the mouse logo was registered with the patents office in London on 25 September 1931. The mouse was carved with a lowered head and the front legs were omitted as they had a tendency to be damaged when the item of furniture was being polished.

The same style of mouse still appears on items of Mouseman furniture today. Stories of curly tails, straight tails, heads to the right and heads to the left relating to different generations running the family business are all mythical, as each and every carved mouse is only an interpretation of what a mouse should look like in the eyes of the craftsmen carving the mouse on the day.

Dining tables

Refectory dining table designs in the 1920s varied, depending very much upon what clients actually required. Some of these early tables were over constructed. I find it hard to believe that great grandfather managed to find the massive oak trees he would have required to make a table with a four or five inch thick top. These large tops were so heavy that it was not necessary to fix them in place. They just sat onto round locating dowels and the actual weight of the top was sufficient to keep them in place.

Such a large piece of furniture would require eight strong men to position. Fine examples of these early Mouseman refectory tables can still be found in use at Ampleforth College and religious establishments around the country today.

In those early years all visible surfaces would display the distinctive rippled adzed finish, with scrolls carved to each corner of the table top. Even the underside of each tabletop would be worked with the adze. This was two fold, as the rough sawn underside to the boards would be adzed smooth at the same time that the top was fitted to the table frame. This was by far the quickest and simplest way for craftsmen to carry out this process until the purchase of a planing machine in the late 1930s.

These early tables would often have solid shaped plank ends with oversized bottom stretchers positioned just above floor level. You will also find that the top two corners of the bottom stretcher will be rounded. This contrasts with the distinctive 45-degree chamfer detail that you will find on the bottom stretchers of refectory tables produced from the 1950s up to the present day.

One of the easiest and most visible ways of dating Mouseman tables is the fox tongue jointing method. This traditional method was used for the joining of single boards together to make up the required width of the table top.

A tongue shaped piece of oak would be inserted into the two adjoining edges that were to be joined together. These were held in place by

four tapered dowels that were driven through offset holes in the tabletop through the loose tongue. This left those four very distinctive dowels showing at every tongue along the length of the table top.

Late in 1971 we ceased using animal glue in the assembly of all of our furniture. Instead, we started using stronger modern adhesives that did not require the fox tongue jointing method to keep the tabletop joints together. Therefore all tables produced from late 1971 to the current day do not have dowels visible in the surface of the top.

Top left:
Dining table
pre-1950.

Top right:
Dining table
1950s to
present day.

Bottom left:
Table top joint
pre 1971.

Bottom right:
Table top joint
post 1971.

To summarise the above:

Tables produced pre 1940s
1. Dowels visible in surface of tabletop.
2. Rounded corners to top of bottom stretcher.
3. All visible surfaces adzed.
4. Underside of table top adzed
5. Carved scrolls to corners of table top.

Tables pre 1950s
1. Dowels visible in surface of table top.
2. Rounded corners to top of bottom stretcher.
3. Adzed on all visible surfaces.

Tables pre 1960s
1. Dowels visible in surface of table top.
2. Chamfered corners at 45 degrees to top of bottom stretcher.
3. Adzed on all visible surfaces.

Tables pre 1971
1. Dowels visible in surface of table top.
2. Chamfered corners at 45 degrees to top of bottom stretcher.
3. Adzed surface to table top and bottom stretcher.

Tables from late 1971 to current day
1. Chamfered corners at 45 degrees to top of bottom stretcher.
2. Adzed surface to table top and bottom stretcher.

Dining Chairs

Over the years we have produced several different styles of chair. The panel back chair as we know it today was great grandfather's original standard dining chair. I believe he designed this chair firstly to go with his early refectory tables that he was producing for the dining halls of the private schools and religious establishments up and down the country. Secondly, it was for the dining rooms of his clients back in the early years.

It was first produced in the 1920s and available both with and without arms. Early examples of this chair would have had front legs spun on a lathe, then worked on at a bench by a craftsman to form that distinctive octagonal shape. They will often retain the telltale 'centre pop' marks where they were held in the lathe. These marks disappeared from the bottom of front legs in the early 1930s from both the dining and the armchairs.

Early examples of this chair can often be seen with a single piece of burr oak as a back panel.

All surfaces on the early chairs were finished with the adze, producing the unique rippled finish. In the 1940s craftsmen leaving to fight in the Second World War and so created a labour shortage. I imagine this was the point when great grandfather made the decision to reduce the man hours it was taking to adze every surface on each chair, so from then on only the chairs' back panels were and still are worked with the adze.

Seats on the very early chairs usually consisted of interwoven thick leather straps that were wrapped around the edge of the four seat rails. They were held in place by flat-headed upholstery tacks to the inside/underside of the four seat rails. This style of seat changed about 1930 to the single solid hide that was attached to the chair in a similar way to its predecessor, the interwoven leather strap seat.

This continued to be the preferred choice of seat until the 1940s. We then see a move to the comfort of an upholstered seat, the very same style that we fit to our range of chairs today. This consists of a drop-in cotton-webbed seat frame with a foam rubber infill, upholstered with a single piece of cow hide held in place by a single row of domed-headed upholstery studs set around the perimeter of the hide covering.

Basic construction of the dining chair today is very similar to those produced back in the early 1920s by my great grandfather. One component that has been re-positioned is the bottom front rail. Originally this structural rail was positioned in between the bottom of the front legs on both the dining and the armchairs. The same rail was removed from between the front legs and re-positioned between the bottom side rails to form what we call in the trade 'rush rail'. The armchairs received this modification first in the mid 1950s. Then in the late '50s the dining chairs received the same modification. This re-positioning from front rail to rush rail enabled a chair to straddle the foot on any one of our dining tables, and also allowed the person seated more leg room.

Top, left to right:

Chair made early 1920s.

Chair 1920s to 1930s.

Chair 1920s to 1930s

Chair 1920s to 1950s

Bottom, left to right:

Chair 1930s to 1940s.

Chair post 1940s.

Chair 1950s to 1970.

Chair 1970 to present day.

To summarise the above:

Chairs produced pre 1930s
1. Adzed all over.
2. Interwoven leather strap seat.
3. Front bottom rail positioned between front legs.
4. 'Centre pop' marks to bottom of octagonal front legs.

Chairs 1930s to mid 1940s
1. Adzed all over.
2. Solid single piece of cow hide for chair seat.
3. Front bottom rail positioned between front legs.

Chairs mid 1940s to 1950s
1. Adzed surface to back panel only.
2. Upholstered cowhide seat held in place with domed-head upholstery nails with cotton webbing clearly visible to underside of seat.

3. Front bottom rail positioned between the two front legs.

Chairs 1950s to 1970
1. Adzed surface to back panel only.
2. Upholstered cowhide seat held in place with domed-headed upholstery nails, with cotton webbing clearly visible to underside of seat.
3. Rush rail positioned between bottom side rails (no front rail between front legs).
4. Carved lattice panels begin to appear in dining and armchairs.

Chairs 1970 to current day
1. Adzed surface to back panel only.
2. Fully upholstered seat.
3. Rush rail reduced in depth to finish below the surface of the bottom side rails.

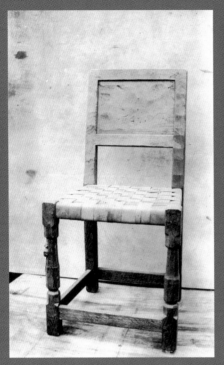

Left: Early panel-back dining chair from the 1920s. The panelling is burr oak and the seat is interwoven leather. This design evolved into a single solid leather seat, and then in the late 1940s and early '50s into today's upholstered seat. The front rail between the legs was later moved back so that the chair could be pushed under the table. When turned upside down, this chair would show centre 'pop' marks from being turned on the lathe.

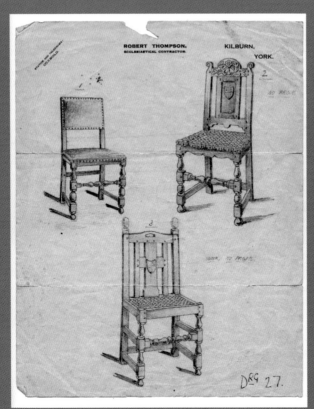

Right: Smoking chair from the early 1930s with cowhide back and interwoven leather seat. It would have a four-inch deep cushion filled with horsehair and also covered in cowhide. Like most early pieces it was adzed all over – a practice reduced in the 1950s because of the labour factor. Such adzing is a great help in dating, and there is a saying at Thompson's that 'the cruder it looks the earlier it was made'.

Bottom: Designs for three chairs, sketched out on a piece of 'ecclesiastical contractor' notepaper that no doubt happened to be at hand. They date from the late 1920s or early '30s when Robert was still experimenting. As can be seen in the top-left corner, it was an age when there was still a railway station at nearby Coxwold and communication was by telegram rather than phone.

Composite group of pieces including an early cheeseboard with the mouse on the board itself. Today it runs down the handle, a change made to add additional strength and prevent breakages. Another change has embraced the fruit bowl at the back of the group, which now has the mouse on the inside. The book trough at the bottom is unusual in that the mouse is running up it. The grain normally makes it slightly easier to carve with the mouse heading downwards.

Collectors please note!

We do not have a precise list of all the subtle changes that have been made to each item of Mouseman furniture throughout the many decades of production and gradual evolution. My sole aim is to give avid collectors the essential details of what to look for so that they can establish a date within a time span of ten years.

Other Pieces

Cheeseboards were first produced back in the 1930s. Early examples were produced with the mouse trademark carved at right angles to the handle and positioned on the board itself. In the 1960s the mouse began to appear carved on the handle of the board. This repositioning of the mouse trademark was due firstly to the strengthening of the handle, as it was found that if the board were accidentally dropped the handle would fracture in the thinnest section. So by moving the mouse onto the handle it helped to strengthen the weakest point. Secondly, carving of the mouse trademark is more difficult across the grain as opposed to along the grain.

Fruit bowls were produced from the 1930s with the mouse trademark originally carved on the outer edge of the bowl. The mouse was repositioned in the 1960s and has appeared carved centrally inside the bottom of the bowl ever since. This change of position enabled the bowl to increase in size from ten inches to about twelve inches in diameter.

GREAT CRAFTSMEN AT WORK

An appreciation by Lord Londonderry

It may seem strange but I had never heard of the Mouseman until the mid-seventies, despite having lived in the North East since 1949. Even though Robert Thompson's had made a plaque to commemorate the modernisation of the school on the family estate at Wynard in 1964 I was still unaware of the Mouseman's existence. It was only ten years later when I was doing research for a book that my eyes were opened. Part of my research involved visiting Rievaulx Abbey and Helmsley, and on the way a friend who was accompanying me told me about the Mouseman and suggested we had a look at the workshops.

The visit turned out to be a revelation. It was the first time I had ever been to a cabinetmaker's workshop and seen great craftsmen at work. The solidity and beauty of the wood, perfectly seasoned English oak, made an instant and lasting impression on me. I immediately resolved to buy some ready-made pieces of furniture and commission others.

Over the years I have bought bookcases, tables, chairs, blanket chests and other sundry items. It even occurred to me to have my coffin made by the Mouseman! Apparently, Robert Thompson's received such requests in the early days of the business. The traditional oblong shape seemed inappropriate, so I settled for a blanket chest. In due course it was delivered to my house and on seeing it I immediately realised it was too good to be used for such a purpose. One of the delivery men agreed with me, saying with brutal honesty that grave robbers would certainly pinch the coffin rather than the corpse!

5 AROUND KILBURN (20 miles)

Coxwold

First stop for many 'mouse seekers' on leaving Kilburn is the nearby village of Coxwold. On entering the village, visitors cannot miss the church of St Michael, which, with its unusual octagonal tower, dominates the wide main street. The church was built between 1420 and 1430 and is considered to be one of the best examples of perpendicular architecture in the former North Riding. Inside are numerous fascinating historical and architectural features: the 18th century box pews were originally rented by local families and were introduced by the parson, Laurence Sterne (of whom, more later); 14th century stained glass in the north nave windows is older than the church itself having been brought from an earlier Norman church; the Royal coat of arms of George II over the chancel arch was introduced to act as a reminder to worshippers that the church belonged to the King rather than the Roman Pope; and superb early 17th, 18th and 19th century monuments trace the history of the local Belasyse family.

For lovers of Mouseman furniture, the church is best known as home to an interesting collaborative work between Robert Thompson and an Austrian wood carver, Joseph Heu. In 1941, fleeing from anti-semitic persecution, Joseph Heu was given refuge and employment by Robert Thompson. Their mutual respect for each other's work came to fruition in a commission for a new lectern at Coxwold church. Robert Thompson carved the pedestal (note the mouse on the base) whilst his Austrian friend and colleague completed the reading desk. Later, Joseph paid a special tribute to his Yorkshire mentor with a carved bas-relief portrait of Robert Thompson (complete with a renegade mouse creeping into his sleeve) that today can be viewed in the museum in Kilburn.

Thompson mice are also evident here in the Lady Chapel, hiding on the simple oak altar and under the ledge of the niche in the wall. A further mouse is to be found on the Bible case, which contains a 'Breeches Bible', printed in 1601. The mice at St Michael's are in good company, as the roof within the church contains some fine examples of mediaeval roof bosses carved with various birds and beasts.

In the church porch is the tombstone of Laurence Sterne, the 18th century author of *Tristram Shandy* and *A Sentimental Journey*, who was vicar at Coxwold from 1760 to 1768. The tombstone was erected in London on Sterne's death in 1768 by a group of Masons. It was removed to Coxwold in 1969 when Sterne's body was re-interred here. His grave is now sited by the south wall of the nave just outside the porch.

The former vicarage, Shandy Hall, is located near the church on the road to Kilburn. It has been painstakingly restored by the Laurence Sterne Trust and provides a step back in time to the days when the amusing parson -

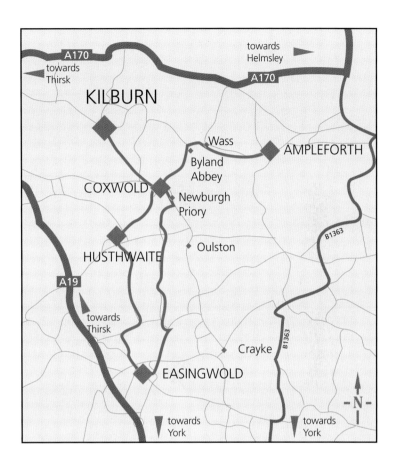

who entertained 18th century London society and was a friend of Hogarth, Garrick and Reynolds - lived quietly there. The house is open to the public and is well worth a visit.

Before leaving the village, visitors may wish to seek refreshment at the Fauconberg Arms, which contains many examples of work by Thompson and his successors. At the village crossroads, the road signs point to the next destination on the Mouse tour, Husthwaite.

Husthwaite

A pleasant drive of just two miles down winding country lanes brings us to Husthwaite. On entering the village turn right into the High Street where St Nicholas' church is found opposite the village green. An original Norman church with later additions, the oak roof was one of Robert Thompson's earliest commissions. Other Mouseman work includes a beautiful traceried altar, lectern, litany desk and reredos. Follow the signs from the village green to Easingwold.

Interior of St Michael's Church, Coxwold.

Inset:
The reading stand at St Michael's Church – a collaboration in 1947 between Joseph Heu and Robert Thompson.

Husthwaite church, where the roof features early work by Robert Thompson in 1920. Other features, such as the altar, lectern and reredos, mainly date from 1935.

Opposite: Just some of the fourteen refectory tables and eighty chairs at Stanbrook Abbey, which are expected to come north as part of the planned relocation to a new monastery on the hillside above Wass.

Easingwold

On entry, the little market town of Easingwold may at first appear unprepossessing but first impressions are deceptive. Following the signs for the market square leads one into a charming cobbled market place, surrounded by 18th and 19th century houses and shops. Driving out of the square and uphill, turn left into Church Hill. Following this road for a few hundred yards, the church of All Saints and St John appears on the right, with its car park opposite.

Described by Nicholas Pevsner as a 'typical North Country church, dark, grey, low and long and without battlements or parapet', this unremarkable exterior hides some fine examples of Mouseman work. Visitors will need to look closely to define the mouse hiding on the High Altar (from 1948) and the Lady Chapel altar. Other Thompson pieces include the reredos behind the high altar, the parclose screen dividing the Lady Chapel from the nave and a credence table.

Turning back down Church Hill towards the junction with Easingwold's main street, proceed straight ahead past pretty cottages and turn left at the next junction. This circular and very scenic route leads past Newburgh Priory on the return to Coxwold. Arriving back at Coxwold, take the road to Ampleforth that passes stunning Byland Abbey, where in 2008 Thompson's provided eight dining tables and thirty-eight chairs for the refurbished dining room at the Abbey Inn.

Wass

The next village is Wass, where there should soon be a striking addition to the long list of buildings with Thompson associations. Nuns at the Benedictine abbey of Stanbrook in Worcestershire are planning to relocate to a new, purpose-built monastery on the edge of the woods above Wass and to bring with them a unique collection of early Mouseman furniture. It includes no less than eighty chairs and fourteen refectory tables completed by Robert Thompson in 1926. Also at Stanbrook is a remarkable pulpit, created by Robert in 1933 to the designs of two members of the community. One of them, Dame Laurentia McLachlan, was described by her good friend George Bernard Shaw as 'an enclosed nun with an unenclosed mind'.

The sisters' relocation will be the first new monastic community to return to North Yorkshire since the reformation during the reign of Henry VIII. The application to build the monastery within the North York Moors National Park gained approval because it accorded with policy to support the spiritual welfare of the area. The scheme includes a monastic guest house for visitors and those seeking contemplative retreats.

Chairs of many kinds, probably photographed when they were supplied to Stanbrook Abbey in 1926. The early monk's chair on the left, with no crossed rail at the bottom, is probably one of the first ever made by Thompson. The remaining chairs have back panels of burr oak and are carved with religious symbols.

The 1926 Thompson pulpit at Stanbrook, bearing the coat of arms of the community's benefactors and the inscription 'Christus Vincit, Christus Regnat, Christus Imperat'.

: SUGGESTIONS for BEDROOM FURNITURE in ENGLISH OAK :

R. Thompson.
Kilburn.
York.

Ampleforth

Continue to Ampleforth, where the Benedictine monastery and school is a mecca not to be missed by Mouseman enthusiasts. As we have seen, it played a pivotal role in the career of Robert Thompson. From that first commission of a crucifix for Father Paul Nevill, extended a personal involvement for Robert Thompson, which lasted for 31 years until his death. Ampleforth contains extensive examples of work by Robert Thompson, including his piece de resistance, the library, which he always referred to as 'my room'. His work in the library started in 1934 with bookcases, carrels (private study desks), chairs, tables and even waste bins. In 1950 he added the immense door. A table in the library bears the inscription 'VPN from RT', testament to his longstanding friendship with Father Paul.

Perhaps to provide some light relief for boys studying within the library's private carrels, Thompson thoughtfully incorporated humorous touches such as comical dragons. laughing heads and, of course, the famous mouse. The mouse here is particularly pleasing, chasing his own tail in a never-ending circle.

The work in the Abbey dates from 1928 and represents Robert Thompson's first commission for Sir Giles Gilbert Scott, one of the most renowned architects of the early 20th century, whose output ranged from the Anglian Cathedral in Liverpool to Bankside Powerstation (now Tate Modern) and the classic red telephone box. Robert Thompson was justly proud of the Abbot's choir stall. On being asked by Sir Giles where he was thinking of making the joins, Robert is reported to have replied: 'Why do you want a join? If you come to me, you can have it in one piece'.

In 1955, Robert Thompson's last and poignant commission at the school was a plaque to commemorate Old Boys who had perished in the Second World War. Today the workshop at Kilburn continues to carry out commissions for the school and monastery, maintaining the relationship that commenced between Father Nevill and Robert Thompson so long ago.

A recent major undertaking was providing the bar, furniture and panelling for the Windmill Social Club. This response to changes in legislation involved a house in the grounds being converted into a licensed club restaurant incorporating a lounge and bistro. Some of the panelling came from a closed accommodation house at the school and was carefully reused.

Ampleforth College is a busy school, and only the works in the Abbey Church are available for viewing by the public and only by prior arrangement. Contact the Hospitality and Pastoral Service Office, telephone 01439 766889. Donations are welcomed.

The preparatory school for Ampleforth is Gilling Castle, a few miles to the south-east on the Helmsley to York road. Robert Thompson was closely involved in the saga of the Elizabethan panelling in the Great Chamber, which is widely considered to be among the finest in Britain. Prior to Ampleforth acquiring the castle, the panelling was bought and removed in the 1930s by the American collector William Randolph Hirst. Fortunately it had only got as far as the docks when war broke out and

Opposite:
This drawing in Robert Thompson's own hand of a plainly furnished bedroom could well represent one of his proposals for Stanbrook Abbey.

*Ampleforth
Abbey church.*

*Opposite:
Interior of the
Abbey church.*

thus Ampleforth was later able to
open a fund to purchase it back.
Robert gave the first donation of £100
on condition that he would re-fit the
panelling – a task he duly and happily
undertook in 1952.

Robert Thompson also provided
the tables and chairs for the refectory
at Gilling. They were liberally adorned
with mice and often featured in
games of 'tig' or 'tick'. A boy touching
a mouse was deemed to be 'safe'.

Above:
Ampleforth College library, which Robert Thompson furnished in 1947–49 and always called 'my room'.

Left:
The 1947 choir stalls in the Abbey church – the first of Robert Thompson's successful collaborations with the eminent architect, Sir Giles Gilbert Scott.

Opposite:
Candle-lit view of a side chapel.

The Windmill Social Club at Ampleforth, where the bar, furniture and panelling has all been provided by Robert Thompson's.

The Great Chamber at Gilling Castle, now a preparatory school for Ampleforth College, where Robert Thompson was closely involved in the saga of its Elizabethan panelling.

6 LOWER RYEDALE (50 miles)

This fifty-mile round trip through beautiful Ryedale countryside takes in some fine examples of Robert Thompson's work in both ecclesiastical and secular surroundings. It also provides opportunity for detours to stunning Rievaulx Abbey and Helmsley Castle.

Helmsley

The little market town of Helmsley nestles among surrounding hills and is bordered by the River Rye. It is the administrative home of the North York Moors National Park and is a popular stopping off point for visitors to the area. Red-roofed houses, shops and wide streets surround the market square where a fine ancient cross contrasts with a Victorian obelisk designed by the eminent architect Sir George Gilbert Scott, whose other works include the Albert Memorial and St Pancras Station in London (as well as St Mary's church in Ambleside, which features in the Lake District 'mouse' tour).

The church of All Saints stands just behind the market square. The lower part of its tower is 13th century whilst the south doorway and chancel arch both bear distinctive Norman zigzag carvings. Look out also for the 11th century hogback stone in the porch.

Inside the church, funerary monuments, stained glass and various historical artefacts provide interest for visitors. Thompson enthusiasts will, however, head straight to the sanctuary where the panelling commemorates those members of the XXII Dragoons who were killed in the Normandy campaigns of 1944/45. The panelling was commissioned by Major Clifford who, with his squadron, was based near Kilburn after the Dunkirk campaign. There he came across Robert Thompson and was so fascinated by the craftsman's skills that he ordered several pieces of furniture for his own home, Frampton Court, a fifteenth century manor house in Gloucestershire. Major Clifford felt obliged to mention to Thompson that his prices were extremely low and that he could charge more if they were sold in London. The craftsman simply replied that he knew he could get more in London but that he preferred to work in his home county, making furniture to order, so that he knew where each piece was going. Also note the altar rails' distinct adzed finish. Inscribed to Walter Baldwin 'peoples' warden' who died in 1926, the mouse runs up the rail post.

Leaving the church, it is just a short walk straight ahead, then turning right opposite the small bridge to the spectacular remains of Helmsley castle, which dates back to around 1200 AD. The remains of a double ditch and the bridge that crossed it can clearly be seen, as can later developments, including two barbicans from the mid 13th century, a 14th century kitchen and 15th century buttery. Elizabethan additions include a fine plaster ceiling and frieze, panelling and an oak fireplace.

The castle started to decline in the late 17th century following its purchase by the Duncombe family and

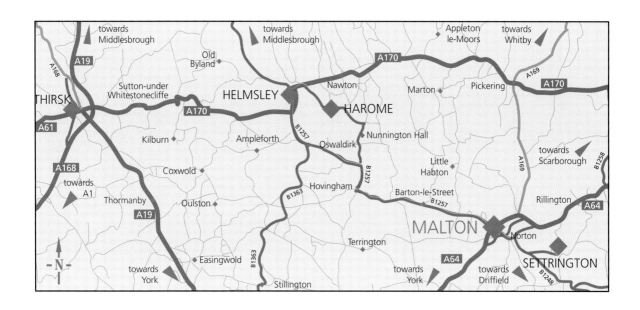

their commissioning of a new building, Duncombe House, the design of which was carried out under the instruction of Sir John Vanburgh.

The landscaped haven of Duncombe Park, complete with temples and terraces, commands superb views of Rievaulx Abbey and Helmsley Castle. Equally stunning views may be obtained from Rievaulx Terrace, a swathe of green nearly half a mile long with temples at each end. The Terrace is now owned by the National Trust.

Just over two miles north-west of Helmsley lies Rievaulx Abbey, the earliest Cistercian abbey in Yorkshire. For many people, the beauty of its setting leaves it rivalled only by Tintern Abbey on the Wye. Visited on a fine summer's day, few would disagree.

Robert Thompson incorporated some attractive carved tracery into his 1930 vestry door in Helmsley church. The wrought-iron handles would be made by a local blacksmith.

Rievaulx Abbey lies in a beautiful setting near Helmsley.

Old Malton

Leaving Helmsley, take the B1257 road towards Malton. Just north of Hovingham is the 16th century manor house, Nunnington Hall now owned by the National Trust and open to the public. Arriving in Old Malton, the church of St Mary is located in the centre of village. Under the west window a carved oak door with traceried panels by Thompson is in complete harmony with the twelfth century doorway that contains it. On the altar, the pulpit and lectern also bear distinctive Thompson carvings and the sign of the mouse. From Malton, follow the B1248 Driffield Road for 2 miles before turning left for Settrington.

Settrington

The picturesque village of Settrington comprises a cluster of red-roofed houses around the sturdy, buttressed 15th century church of All Saints. Inside the church, the litany desk and organ seat are particularly fine examples of Robert Thompson's work. There are numerous other architectural features both inside and outside the church which will tempt the visitor to linger a while. Look out particularly for the 12th century font and, outside, at the 13th century zigzag and floral carvings over the south doorway arch. Casting an eye skywards to the top of the tower reveals some interesting carved heads and an unusual kneeling figure with a man behind.

Harome

From Settrington, retrace your steps to Malton and Hovingham, from there follow signposts to Nunnington and Harome. Here the Star Inn not only provides a pleasant opportunity for refreshment but also contains some attractive early pieces of Thompson furniture.

Suitably refreshed, visitors now have only a short drive back to Helmsley.

7 EAST YORKSHIRE (70 miles)

This 70 mile journey offers something for everyone: the busy shops and architectural heritage of Beverley; the gentle scenery of the Wolds and the bracing sea air of Bridlington.

Beverley

In terms of ecclesiastical heritage and Thompson's art, the small town of Beverley has an embarrassment of riches. In the 1940s, Arthur Mee, in his review of The King's England, described the town as 'an exquisite beauty, unsurpassed in Yorkshire. York Minster is not more lovely than Beverley Minster, and as if that were not enough for a small town, here is the beautiful church of St Mary to keep it company'. Both churches are also central to this Thompson tour and the work in each commemorates the fallen of the 1939-45 war.

At the Minster, which is considered to be one of the finest Gothic buildings in Europe, Thompson's work is to be found within the Military Chapel. Here the altar rails, chairs, entrance screen, Book of Remembrance and the door to the staircase are all fine examples of Mouseman work. Each of the chairs is dedicated to a fallen soldier and all bearing the mouse in silent witness. Those wishing to complete this particular Mouseman tour in one day will have little time to linger within the Minster although it would be a shame to miss the choir with its unique misericords. This brief encounter will no doubt persuade many to return another day to do full justice to the truly impressive interior.

The short walk from the Minster to St Mary's allows visitors to take in some of the sights of this charming town. The narrow streets reveal a hotchpotch of architectural styles, all contained within the remains of an ancient ditch and a palisade with five gates, one of which the North Bar, dating from 1409, has been restored.

At St Mary's, the oak door acts as a war memorial. Designed by the architect, Leslie Temple Moore, it was commissioned during Robert Thompson's lifetime but was completed after this death by his grandsons. The panels bear the names of fallen parishioners. The mouse may be seen lurking at the right hand base of the door.

Whilst in the church, look out for another animal of interest - a statue of a hare dressed in man's clothes - it is said to have provided Lewis Carroll with his inspiration for the White Rabbit in Alice in Wonderland.

To take in all the sights that Beverley has to offer would easily occupy a full day but Bridlington and the sea beckon.

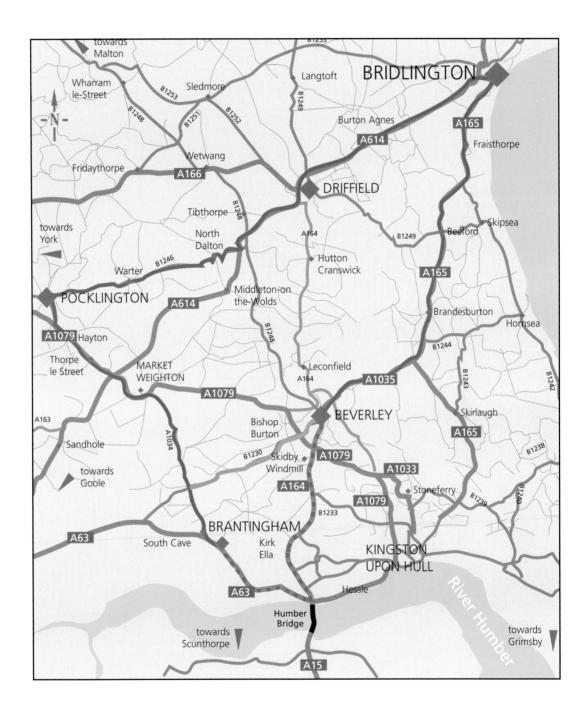

Aerial view of Beverley Minster, one of the finest Gothic buildings in Europe, which contains several examples of Thompson work in its Military Chapel.

Bridlington

Leaving Beverley on the A1035 road it is a 20 mile journey north east to Bridlington or "Brid' as it is popularly known: and Bridlington is popular. Its heyday, like so many other English seaside towns, may have passed but Bridlington still offers much for lovers of the sea. The South Bay has a particularly fine stretch of sand for bathers and offers all the usual seaside family attractions. The picturesque quay by the waterfront is linked to the original Old Town inland by a stretch of Victorian buildings which followed the coming of the railway to cater for the new wave of Victorian holiday makers. The town is rich in maritime history - it was here that the ship carrying Charles Stuart's queen sought refuge from the pursuing Roundheads - and aeronautical history too, with the interesting Amy Johnson Collection at nearby Sewerby Hall. So there is much to detain visitors in Bridlingon but for Mouseman enthusiasts, the focus of the visit is the Priory Church of St Mary the Virgin in the Old Town.

The church is all that remains of a great Augustinian monastery founded at the beginning of the 12th century by Walter de Gant. Following the dissolution of the monasteries under Henry VIII, the nave was all that was allowed to remain standing. This too eventually fell into ruin until it was restored in the 1870s by Sir George Gilbert Scott.

St Mary's has many superb examples of Robert Thompson's work including two stalls in the chancel. These bear exact reproductions of carvings made in 1519 by William Bromflet of Ripon, the mediaeval master wood carver whose work in Ripon Cathedral provided the young Robert Thompson with his original creative inspiration.

Other late Thompson work within St Mary's includes the war memorial screens (another design by Leslie Temple Moore), the font canopy (1955), and the parclose screen gates to the sanctuary (1949). The pulpit panelling, canopy and spiral staircase, were added in 1960 to a much older stone pulpit. The Thompson carving is highly ornate, including representations of viking ships and scenes from the life of Christ. Other smaller items are also found here, including a sanctuary chair and prie-dieu, a table at the west end of the church and a lectern stool. In the Bayle Gate Upper Room are a number of large, adzed refrectory tables.

Leaving the sea, the Mouseman trail now follows the A614 past Driffield and then the B1246 across the Wolds to Pocklington.

Opposite:
An oak door at St Mary's Church, Beverley, acts as a war memorial. Commissioned during Robert Thompson's lifetime, it was completed after his death by his grandsons. John Cartwright is seen gilding one of the shields in 1955.

Pocklington

Coming down from the Wolds, Pocklington appears on the plain below - a picturesque market town with an imposing mediaeval church at its centre. The village was the home of the 18th century anti-slavery campaigner, William Wilberforce, who was educated in the old grammar school here. The church, known as the 'cathedral of the Wolds', has Norman foundations, a few elements of which remain including a font bowl. However, the major part of the church, including the imposing tower, comprises 15th century additions. There are fascinating carvings of gargoyles and men's faces both inside and outside the church. Here, visitors can literally play 'cat and mouse' by seeking out the Norman carving of a cat's head in the porch and Thompson's trademark rodent on the altar rails. Leaving Pocklington on the Market Weighton road (the A1079) the nearby gardens of Burnby Hall offer an attractive diversion especially for lovers of water lilies - the gardens are renowned for their lily ponds.

On past Market Weighton and then along the A1034 South Cave road to Brantingham.

Brantingham

At the church in this small village, Thompson's work is represented by two unusual wooden crosses in the churchyard, which commemorate members of the Massey family. The mouse may be found on each cross.

The church combines a mediaeval tower with Norman foundations. The south doorway is 12th century and the interesting font inside is only slightly younger.

Retrace your route through South Cave, from where it is only 10 miles back to Beverley via the B1230.

Alternatively follow the A63 towards the Humber Bridge and then the A164 back to Beverly, passing Skidby Windmill along the way. Built in 1821, Skidby is the last working windmill north of of the Humber. It is open to the public at weekends and Wednesday to Sunday in the summer.

Opposite: Bench end in Bridlington Priory church, made by Robert Thompson in 1947 as an exact reproduction of mediaeval stalls originally carved in 1519 by William Bromflet of Ripon.

8 AINSTY COUNTRY (35 Miles)

The city of York provides an excellent starting and finishing point for this short tour which, in a thirty five-mile round trip, reveals some hidden gems of Mouseman carvings. The tour allows visitors to explore quiet backwater villages, which are so often overlooked by drivers speeding along the busy A64 to and from York.

Bishopthorpe

The village of Bishopthorpe lies just 2 miles south of York close to the famous racecourse. On first entering the village, it appears quiet and unassuming and it is something of a shock, therefore, to come across Bishopthorpe Palace, the present home of the Archbishop of York. The Palace is not open to the public but the view from the entrance gate of the main building, fronted by manicured lawns, presents an idyllic picture.

The church of St Andrew is just across the road from the Palace. The pale stonework of the church is half covered in ivy and creepers, and in summer is framed all around by a border of 'cottage garden' flowers. Visitors may rest awhile on benches thoughtfully provided to allow one to soak up the atmosphere of this almost perfect English village church.

Inside the church, the work of Robert Thompson is immediately presented in the form of the magnificent, eight sided, pinnacled font cover. Designed by G G Pace, it is suspended over the ancient stone font, which was transferred to the church, along with the two church bells, from the much older church of St Crux in York. The carved mouse appears immediately above the start of the inscription to Augusta Anne Maclaglan 'a faithful worshipper in the church' who died in 1908.

Whilst in the church, take time to view the stained glass windows which depict interesting scenes from the village's history including Archbishop de Gray repealing the Game Law in 1226 and King Charles I's visit of 1633. One of the most loved windows is the 'school window' which was presented in memory of a former school teacher. It depicts four class room scenes from 1350, 1693, 1846 and finally, 1950.

On leaving the church, take a walk on past the Palace and then turn left down Chantry Lane. This leads to the riverside and the site of the former parish church of St Andrew, now marked by a stone cross where the altar once stood. Ancient tombs from the graveyard are stacked against the wall and make fascinating reading. Past the riverbank comes a constant stream of pleasure craft and tourist cruisers, on their way to and from the city of York.

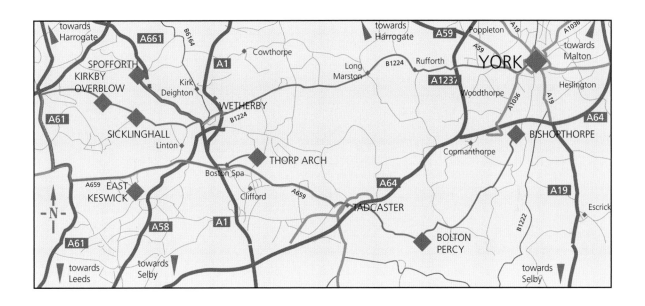

Thompson furniture in Bishopthorpe church includes this faldstool with pierced tracery, shields on the carved front and an inscription plus floral motifs on the heavily carved ends.

Bolton Percy

Returning to the car, follow the road signs to Copmanthorpe and Bolton Percy, reached in five miles. The church which dates from the early 15th century is a fine example of the perpendicular style. It dominates the village green and is indicative of the former importance of the village as a trading centre and river thoroughfare.

Robert Thompson carved the lych gate which bears an inscription of Samuel Smith of Oxton Hall who died in 1927. A well-worn figure of St Oswald guards the entrance to the lych gate. Visitors may spend some time looking for the Thompson mouse as it is not easy to find (the photograph accompanying this section gives a clue!).

The interior of this church is fascinating; the box pews are Jacobean as is the smaller of the two pulpits; the larger pulpit is Caroline. The East window above the altar is also of interest, being the only remaining mediaeval glass in which Mary, the Blessed Virgin, is prominent.

Mousework is manifest in the altar rails. These are very plain and are not in the usual obviously adzed finish. The mouse symbol is found inset on the inside of the left-hand altar rail as one looks at the altar. The mouse also appears creeping along the edge of the hymn number box. Two standard candle sticks, dedicated to H S Woolcombe are no longer on the altar but are kept inside the vestry.

On leaving the church, cross the road to the side of the church and enter the cemetery garden through an iron gate. Inside this walled garden is a riotous tumult of flowers in the summer almost obscuring the tombstones within.

Before leaving the village, a walk round to the other side of the church leads to the Crown Inn. A pleasant garden leads down to the river, which is crossed by a narrow wooden footbridge.

Thorp Arch

On leaving Bolton Percy, follow the signs for Tadcaster, there turn right in the town centre to take the A659 towards Wetherby through Boston Spa. In the centre of Boston Spa, turn right following the sign for the British Library, crossing the arched stone bridge over the wide river. Travelling up the hill, the church of All Saints appears on the right after a couple of hundred yards. The church is usually locked, so it may be advisable to phone ahead.

Inside the church, all the woodwork is by Thompson apart from the altar which comes from the Austrian town of Oberammergau, famous for its mediaeval passion play. The majority of the Thompson work here dates from 1935 and was considered by Thompson to be among his best work, notably the pulpit, two carved screens and pews.

Whilst the honey coloured stone houses of Thorp Arch present a pretty picture, there is little else in the village to detain the visitor and so retrace the route back to Boston Spa village. Follow the signs for Collingham, where bear right onto the A659 Harewood road. Just outside Collingham, a left turn leads to East Keswick where St Mary's church has a large collection of Thompson work dating from the 1955 to 1962 period.

Go back to the A659 and at the

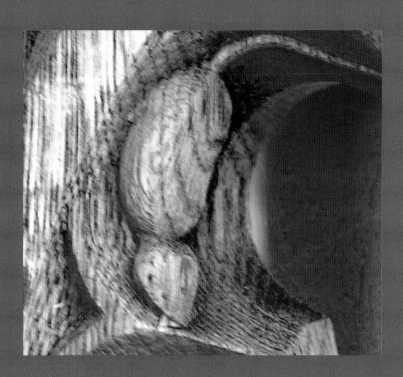

traffic lights in Harewood turn right onto the busy A61 linking Leeds with Harrogate. After crossing the River Wharfe look out for a right-hand turn to Kirkby Overblow, where All Saints Church has an altar, table and stool from 1940.

Sicklinghall

Follow signs for Sicklinghall and travel up the hill that forms the main street. The Catholic church of Mary Immaculate is found on the left. Inside, mice are to be found everywhere; on the pews, the tables at the back of church, the altar rails, panelling and screen. Even the Stations of the Cross are the work of the mouseman. The church continues to purchase Thompson furniture, some of its latest pieces including a Pascal candlestick in memoriam of Reginald Morton Holmes (1998) who was a great supporter of the church and a lover of mouseman furniture.

The Catholic church of Mary Immaculate at Sicklinghall, which continues to purchase Thompson furniture.

Opposite: The lych gate for Bolton Percy church assembled outside Thompson's workshop prior to installation.

Spofforth

From Sicklinghall, retrace the route back to the outskirts of Wetherby and turn sharp left onto the A661 for Spofforth. Here the church of All Hallows contains one of Robert Thompson's last works, a board recording the names of the church's rectors. Other Thompson pieces include the lectern, rector's stall, choir stall and altar rails.

Whilst in the churchyard, look out for the grave of John Metcalfe, otherwise known as 'Blind Jack of Knaresborough' who despite losing his sight as a small boy, built up a national reputation as a roadmaker.

From Spofforth, head back to Wetherby and then pick up the B1224 out of Wetherby and it is 12 miles back to York. You will pass through Long Marston village, the site of the battle of Marston Moor in 1644.

LOWER WHARFEDALE (35 miles)

The busy towns of Harrogate and Ilkley are ideal starting and finishing points for this circular tour. Both are well equipped with shops, refreshment places, museums and natural beauty to ensure that this short tour provides a full and varied day's amusement for the most discerning visitor. For Thompson enthusiasts, this tour is particularly interesting as it includes some of the craftsman's very last ecclesiastical work and examples of his fruitful collaboration with his friend, the architect J S Symes.

Harrogate

Fashionable boutiques, antique emporia, numerous cafés, hotels, museums and other tourist attractions are all contained within one of the loveliest towns in northern England. The cafés include the famous Betty's tea rooms, where Thompson's have fitted out the private boardroom above the shop and made a large cabinet to house a collection of teapots. They have also provided an eleven-foot long table, twelve padded-back hide chairs, four smoking chairs, a coffee table, sideboard and display cabinet for a meeting room (also private) at Betty's Bakery in nearby Starbeck

Harrogate's popularity, which started to grow in the 1570s, really took off in 1848 with the coming of the railway. Visitors flocked to sample the supposed health giving properties of the waters at numerous wells in and around the town. At the height of its popularity, it attracted royalty and aristocracy from all over Europe. In 1926 it was in the spotlight as the hiding place of crime writer Agatha Christie whose mysterious 'disappearance' attracted huge media coverage and public interest. The famous Pump Room in the centre of the town is now a museum and allows visitors a fascinating glimpse of the Spa in its heyday. At the Pump Room, visitors can also sample the waters, the sulphurous smell of which will appeal only to those of the strongest constitution. In the centre of the town, the famous Stray - 200 acres of open grassland and trees - provides excellent picnicking opportunities, as does the Valley Gardens with its delightful floral displays and pathways. For those who prefer to take their relaxation indoors, the town's famous Turkish Baths, in all their Victorian splendour, are a real treat.

Two churches close to the centre of the town contain fine examples of Thompson work. The first, Christ Church, appears as a grey stone outcrop among the grassy acres of The Stray, to the south east of the town centre, close to the junction of York Place and Skipton Road.

The church was constructed in 1831 at a cost of £4,500, much of it donated by wealthy benefactors, many of whom were visitors to Harrogate. The memorials inside the church and in the graveyard give a poignant insight into the large number of people who came to Harrogate from outside the region

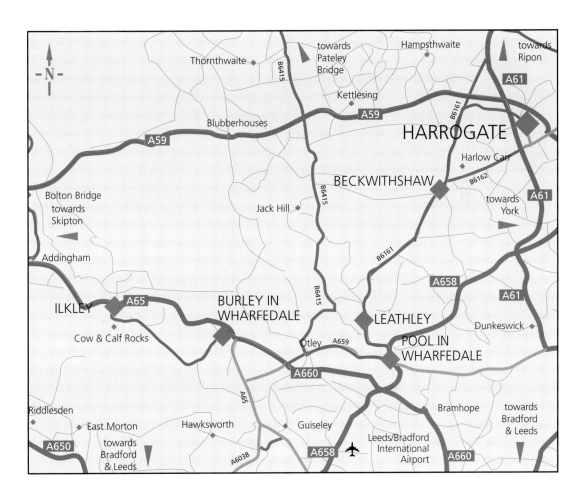

(and from abroad) presumably hoping for a cure and yet who ended their days in the town.

But there are also happier stories to be found inside the church, including one commemorated by Thompson – the altar rails, which are very early Thompson, were commissioned by the vicar, Canon Guy, in thanks for the safe return of his four sons from the Great War. The mouse can be found inside both the left and right rail.

To discover more church mice in Harrogate, head now for St Wilfrid's. Proceed back to the town centre to Parliament Street and out past the Turkish Baths on the road to Ripon. The fourth road on the left is Duchy Road. Turn down here and St Wilfrid's, a yellow stone church, is found a short distance on the left. The choir stalls are Thompson's along with a table in the north chapel. In the nave, three kneelers in front of the screen bear recessed mice and in the Lady chapel, two kneelers are 'mouseman' dated 1941.

Herbert Beaver
born June 5th
died June 6th
1797

Beckwithshaw and Leathley

It is now time to leave Harrogate and discover more of Thompson's work in Lower Wharfedale. Leaving St Wilfrid's church, carry on along Duchy Road, turning right at the end of the road along Harlow Moor Road. Follow this road over a small stone bridge until it meets the B6161, Otley road, where our next destination, Pool, is sign-posted left 8 miles. A short distance on, at Beckwithshaw village, you will pass signs to the Royal Horticultural Society's Harlow Carr Gardens. These comprise 68 acres of landscaped and themed gardens as well as a branch of Betty's Tearooms. St Michael and All Angels at Beckwithshaw has a Thompson font cover and litany desk from 1948.

Leave the village and cross open countryside with delightful long-distance views to reach Leathley. The large and relatively recent Thompson collection in St Oswald's church has many items dating from the late 1960s. These include choir stalls, a lectern, litany desk and font cover.

Pool in Wharfedale

Continue across the River Wharfe to Pool. This small village is centred on the convergence of several roads, linking Leeds, Skipton, Harrogate and Bradford. Apart from the fine views across the river to Leathley and Farnley - a base for artist J M W Turner during his tour of the north – there is little to detain the visitor here apart from the Methodist chapel where some of Robert Thompson's last work is found. The pieces within the chapel, including the pulpit, reredos, communion rails and table, were all completed in 1955, the year of Thompson's death. They also represent some of the final pieces in a long and fruitful artistic partnership between the Kilburn craftsman and a York architect, J S Syme. Further examples of this happy collaboration will be found at this tour's final destination, Ilkley. But first, on to Burley in Wharfedale.

Burley in Wharfedale

Travelling to Burley in Wharfedale from Pool, one may choose to take either the top road (A660 towards Ilkley) which skirts the foot of the Chevin and offers fantastic long distance views along the Wharfe Valley or alternatively a lower road (A659) following the banks of the River Wharfe and through the centre of Otley. The former is more dramatic in terms of scenery whilst the latter offers a chance to sample the sights and sounds of the busy, unpretentious market town of Otley.

Both routes eventually merge on the far side of Otley and from here it is now a straight run on a new road to Burley in Wharfedale. Approaching Burley, the blue clock face on the spire of St Mary the Virgin, is clearly seen and this pinpoints the location of our next Thompson destination. Entering the village, the church is found on the right, opposite the village green.

Inside, Thompson's distinctive style makes the altar rails immediately recognisable as his work, which is just as well as the trademark mouse will not be found here should one seek it as a clue. There was a mouse once, but it is said that a lady parishioner, of nervous disposition but undoubtedly of great influence, objected to having

Opposite:
Top:
Christ Church, an oasis amid Harrogate's famous Stray, has some very early Thompson altar rails.

Middle:
Gravestones outside Ilkley parish church.

Bottom:
Robert Thompson (left) with his lifelong friend, the architect J S Syme, at Ilkley parish church in 1953. The organ cases here were one of their last joint ventures.

to kneel next to it and it was duly removed! Other Robert Thompson pieces (all dating from the early 1950s) include the choir stalls, clergy stalls, pulpit and altar riddel posts. Later work, completed by the company after Robert Thompson's death, is represented by a lectern from the 1970s.

From Burley village to Ilkley, there is again a choice of a low road by the side of the River Wharfe, or a high road, skirting the Moor. This time, the long distance views from on high, make the latter the better choice.

In the centre of Burley village, turn left at the mini roundabout, sign-posted to the station. The road leads up through Burley Woodhead towards the moor. At the top of the road, turn right and follow this road in the direction of Ilkley. You are now skirting the famous Ilkley Moor, part of the South Pennine Moors, designated as a site of special scientific interest. The moor is renowned for its bird life including curlew, golden plover, peregrine and merlin – all are shy birds and visitors are more likely to see wood pigeons and grouse, which are plentiful on the moor.

The road rises steeply, offering superb long distance views along the Wharfe Valley. On a clear day you can see for miles; when it is misty, the eerie qualities of the wilderness are heightened; on a winter's day, the snow-covered moor is breathtaking. In fact, whatever, the weather, this drive will enchant even the most weary traveller. The real drama of the tour is reached at the famous Cow and Calf Rocks. These mighty boulders perch precariously on the edge of the moor and offer a dramatic practice ground for rock climbers. Turning the corner by the rocks, the view opens up into a quite breathtaking panorama with Ilkley town spread out below and views way up the dale beyond. The road now drops sharply into the town centre.

Ilkley

Ilkley is almost always immediately associated with the Yorkshire anthem 'On Ilkla Moor baht 'at'. A walk on the moor is recommended for anyone interested in natural history, geology, Bronze Age stone carvings or, of course, simply to blow the cobwebs away. Ilkley also has much to offer down in the town. In Roman times, the town - known as Olicana - was a strategic base and crossing point of the Wharfe. The town's museum, which is housed in the old manor house, is built on the site of the Roman fort and contains interesting Roman artifacts and reconstructions of the fort. The museum also provides a potted history of the town after the departure of the Romans, including its Victorian heyday as a spa town built around the supposed curative powers of the moorland spring up at White Wells. Today, many of the town's former hydropathic institutes are hotels or retirement homes. The sight of these imposing, ivy-clad buildings allows one's mind to wander back to a time when 'water cures' and a restorative stay in Ilkley were the height of fashion among polite society.

Just next to the Manor House museum is the parish church of All Saints, also built on the site of the Roman fort of Olicana. The present building is partly mediaeval but was largely re-built in Victorian times.

Inside, Thompson enthusiasts and organ lovers alike will be fascinated with the organ cases, which were a collaborative effort between Robert Thompson and the architect and designer, J S Syme of York. The cases won the Organ Club's prize for the best new organ cases when they were completed in 1953 - they were also one of the last major commissions carried out by Robert Thompson himself. It is interesting to note that the mouse on each of these pieces is recessed rather than carved in relief. This was to deter souvenir hunters who at that time were 'bagging' Thompson mice much to the annoyance of Robert Thompson and the owners of the furniture.

There are many other points of interest in the church including the 13th Century doorway with distinctive dogtooth moulding. Earlier still are the exquisitely carved Saxon crosses, the presence of which indicate that Ilkley must have been an important ecclesiastical centre in Anglo-Saxon times. Oak boxed pews and the font from the 17th century are also of interest as is the effigy of Sir Adam Middelton, a member of the dominant Middelton clan whose ancient family seat can be seen overlooking the town.

From the Parish Church, head up Brook Street, the town's main thoroughfare. At the top of the street, take Wells Road, which rises steeply towards Ilkley Moor.

Visitors with time to spare may wish to carry on to the top of Wells Road and then walk up to White Wells, the ancient bathhouse into which an ice-cold moorland spring emerges. Once teams of donkeys carried invalids and visitors to this primitive plunge-pool, which was recommended as a cure for all types of ailments. Today, the hardy (or foolhardy) may immerse themselves in the chilly waters on New Year's Day. The building is open most days – look to see if the flag is flying over the building. From White Wells, the views are magnificent: across to Barden Moor up the Wharfe Valley or back towards Otley and Leeds, they make it well worth the steep walk and highlight Ilkley's position as the gateway to the Dales.

Halfway up Wells Road, look out for three stone steps which mark the site of an old donkey station. Turn right here onto Queens Road and St Margaret's Church is a couple of hundred yards along on the left. Here are found Thompson's mice on the altar rails, candlesticks, chairs in the lady chapel and on a memorial board to previous vicars.

Across the road from the church is a large enclosed stone, upon which may be seen bronze age carvings similar to those found on Ilkley Moor.

Leaving Ilkley, the route continues on the A65 in the direction of Skipton, through Addingham, on towards Bolton Bridge and over Blubberhouses Moor. At the top of the moor, the unsuspecting visitor receives a jolt with the surreal juxtaposition of space age technology and natural wilderness at the US Airbase at Menwith Hill. In fact, no matter how many times one passes the site, the huge white 'golf balls' never fail to fascinate. After Menwith it is just a short drive into Harrogate and the end of a varied and stimulating day's tour.

10 THE UPPER DALES (70 miles)

This tour is crammed full of history and also takes in some of the most scenic areas of Wharfedale, Nidderdale and Swaledale. En route, visitors will discover Thompson's work brushing shoulders with Saxon remains at Ripon Cathedral and military artifacts at the Green Howards museum in Richmond.

It also allows visitors to pay homage to two Yorkshire 'greats': William Bromflet, the mediaeval woodcarver whose work in Ripon Cathedral so inspired the young Robert Thompson; and the much loved Yorkshire writer, J B Priestley, whose final resting place is to be found in the quiet graveyard at Hubberholme. Other historical 'personalities' encountered on this tour include Lewis Carroll and Mary Queen of Scots.

Ripon

The cathedral church of St Peter and St Wilfrid dominates the picturesque huddle of ancient buildings and winding streets that make up Ripon, one of the smallest cathedral cities in England. The cathedral's Saxon crypt was founded by St Wilfrid in 672 AD whilst the main building was built between 1154 and 1530.

Before seeking Thompson's work in the cathedral, visitors should first seek out the misericords in the choir carved by William Bromflet and his school, between 1489 and 1494. Bromflet's carvings were an inspiration for Thompson and help to place his work in context.

The Ripon misericords present finely carved depictions of well known biblical scenes, merged with secular images - such as hunting scenes - and pagan or mythical figures, which combine to provide a fascinating insight into the life and psyche of mediaeval folk. Detailed descriptions and explanations of all the misericord carvings are provided by the cathedral. Look out particularly on the north side for the dancing pigs, playing bagpipes; St Cuthman wheeling his aged mother in a wheel barrow; and the 'pelican' shedding its own blood to feed its children, perhaps never having seen a pelican, the carver's image is closer to that of a swan. On the south side, a carving of a fox preaching to a goose is a satirical depiction of travelling friars and other unscrupulous clerics. At the end of this row, is a picture of a rabbit caught by a griffin whilst in the background another rabbit disappears down its burrow. This image is famed as Lewis Carroll's inspiration for Alice in Wonderland - his father was Cannon of Ripon from 1852 to 1868.

We shall meet up again with Lewis Carroll (and fantasy animals) later in the tour in Richmond.

Having examined Bromflet's work, visitors will be eager to compare it with Thompson's. The Kilburn craftsman's early work is demonstrated in St Wilfrid's chapel (close to the north door) by a pair of tall candlesticks with blue coloured decoration. Produced in the 1920s, these are without the mouse trademark and yet are immediately

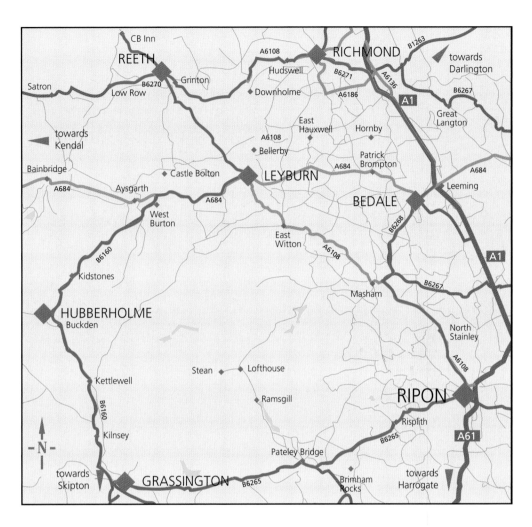

identifiable by the rugged, adzed finish. A further set of slightly smaller candlesticks, dated 1937, 1942 and c.1945 are now used for funeral services. Stored in the Chapter House, they are not readily available for public viewing.

As Thompson gave new life to the style and technique of Bromflet, so too the 'Mouseman's' tradition was continued in the cathedral by his successors. In the library, at the top of the wooden stairs is a long, low cupboard with four panelled doors. The mouse is clearly seen at the front on the left leg. A memorial plaque confirms its date of 1969 and its partner, a desk, is located at the information station near the north door. Also at the north door reception, is a fine chair with a curved back and webbed leather seat, it bears the head of a ram and another beast at the end of each arm. A partner chair also exists in the Chapter House.

In addition to the work of Bromflet and Thompson, there is much to admire in the cathedral. Visitors with limited time will be rewarded by a visit to the Treasury (a small entrance fee is payable) which contains the Saxon 'Ripon Jewel'. This

Ripon Cathedral dominates one of the smallest of all cathedral cities.

The interior of Ripon Cathedral provided Robert Thompson with much of his early inspiration.

Some of the mediaeval misericords from Ripon cathedral that inspired the young Robert Thompson.

Opposite: Carved bench end at Ripon Cathedral. This picture is from a large collection of photographs of mediaeval carvings, which Thompson used as references in his own work.

small but exquisite roundel was found in 1976 close to the cathedral. It is dated to the time of St Wilfrid (c670 AD) and was probably made as a decoration for a relic casket or cross.

Also of interest and dating from the earliest period of the cathedral's history is the crypt. The vaulted stone ceiling in the main chamber is unique in England.

Leaving the cathedral, visitors may wish to explore the streets, shops and museums of Ripon before returning to the car to continue the tour.

From Ripon, take the B6265 road to Pateley Bridge. One quickly comes upon the walls of Studley Royal Park and Fountains Abbey. Here are found the most complete remains of a Cistercian abbey in Britain as well as spectacular 18th century landscaped gardens and a deer park. There is a full and diverse programme of activities in the Park all year round, phone ahead for details.

Continuing on into Nidderdale, the road leads over moorland and past signs to Brimham Rocks. The rocks, which are situated just over a mile from the main road, have been weathered into dramatic shapes, presenting a weird, slightly sinister atmosphere.

The main road starts to drop down into the busy, riverside town of Pateley Bridge, which offers a wide range of simple, countryside tourist attractions. A steep climb on the B6265 road from Nidderdale to Wharfedale, goes over Greenhow to Grassington, a suitable 'half-way house' between Ripon and our next 'Mouseman' location, Hubberholme.

Grassington

This delightful Dales village is a mecca for tourists and can be quite crowded in the Summer. Nonetheless, its narrow cobbled streets and market square retain a simple 'olde worlde' charm. Park in the main car park, which is also the site for the National Park information centre and is just a few hundred yards from the village centre. In the village are all the usual amenities plus interesting craft and antique shops that one expects in a tourist honey-pot.

For history lovers, Grassington offers a great deal and first stop must be the folk museum situated right in the market square. From the village centre, there are also a number of walks of historic interest including up on to Grassington Moor where relics of the village's lead mining heritage may be found. Other footpaths lead to the sites of Bronze Age and Iron Age settlements and include the finest example of a Celtic field system in the Dales.

From the car park, in the opposite direction to the village centre, it is just a short walk down to the river where the tumbling waters of Linton Falls are crossed by the 'Tin Bridge'. A pretty walk past the redundant Linton Mill, by the riverside cottages and along to Linton church provides an opportunity for drivers to stretch their legs and enjoy the bird song and natural beauty of this secluded beauty spot. Then it is back to the car park and off again to Hubberholme.

Hubberholme

From Grassington, the trail (B6160) leads up the Wharfe Valley to Buckden and onto Hubberholme. The church of St Michael and All Angels sits on the banks of the Wharfe and is distinguished for having one of the few rood lofts left in Yorkshire. It is also famed as the final resting place of the great Yorkshire author, J B Priestley, whose ashes are buried here. Inside, Thompson's skills are demonstrated in the pews and choir stalls, completed in 1933 and 34.

Having recrossed the river to the church, continue on the unclassified road and rejoin the B6160 at Cray. Turn left and accompany the gurgling beck down Bishopdale to the picturesque village of West Burton. On meeting the A684, turn right for the market town of Leyburn. A detour can be made at this point to Aysgarth Falls to see the foaming waters of the River Ure and Bolton Castle where Mary Queen of Scots was imprisoned.

Opposite:
Top:
Fountains Abbey, between Ripon and Pateley Bridge, is the most complete Cistercian foundation in Britain.

Left:
The main street of Pateley Bridge, a pleasant town beside the River Nidd.

Right:
Hubberholme church has pews and choir stalls completed by Robert Thompson in 1933 and '34.

Leyburn

Leyburn has a no-nonsense, down-to-earth appearance and is no less attractive for it. Comprising mainly Georgian and Victorian stone buildings around the market square, the town is steeped in history. The main street is expansive to accommodate its Friday market - an institution here since it moved to the town in the 1680s when the dominant market town of Wensley was decimated by the plague.

The Parish Church of St Matthew is passed on the right as one enters the town. Due to its location on this main road, it is perhaps easier to drive on a short distance and park in the Market Place and then walk back to the church, built in 1868. Inside, Thompson's work is revealed in the form of the lectern, pulpit and prie-dieu, dating from 1940 to 1946.

Time may now necessitate continuing on the main road to Richmond, but an attractive detour is to head across the moors and enter spectacularly beautiful Swaledale at Reeth. Two nearby inns under the same ownership have recently installed Mouseman furniture. It has been provided in the bar area at Low Row's Punch Bowl Inn and in a new conference and function facility at Arkengarthdale's CB Inn. The road between the two hostelries is briefly submerged in a shallow moorland beck, made famous as the ford in the opening sequence of the James Herriot TV classic All Creatures Great and Small.

From Reeth head down Swaledale. Passing through Downholme, the route follows the course of the river through a dramatic steep-sided, craggy faced and heavily wooded valley, leading to Richmond.

Richmond

The ancient market town of Swaledale is dominated by the brooding presence of its Norman castle. Open to the public, the castle's parapets, and the promenade round the castle exterior provide fantastic long distance views. In the town the winding streets offer something of interest at every turn, including a beautifully preserved Georgian theatre.

The history of Richmond is intertwined with that of the Green Howards, one of Britain's oldest and most famous army regiments. Thompson's work is located within the regimental chapel (in the church of St Mary the Virgin) and in the regimental museum, which is located in the town's market square.

Head first for the church, which is located on the outskirts of the town centre about five minutes' walk from the market place. The exact date of the church's foundation is unknown but it certainly dates back before 1147. However, it was subject to extensive modernisation work in 1857. Before entering the church, it is interesting to explore the churchyard which includes a number of fascinating graves including, on the north side of the church, the plague stone which marks the site of a communal grave. The churchyard also offers us another link to Charles Lutwidge Dodgson (better known as Lewis Carroll) who played here whilst a pupil at Richmond School from 1844. Inside the church, the misericords under the seats in the choir are worthy of note. These seats were brought to the church from nearby Easby Abbey following the dissolution of the monasteries. Some of the carvings - the bagpipe-playing

Design for an oak fender for the Green Howards, with the cap badge on the front. Thought to be just pre-1939.

FRONT ELEVATION

The Green Howards' Chapel at St Mary the Virgin, Richmond, includes this striking depiction of Calvary as a Second World War battlefield. It is one of Thompson's most unusual and memorable works.

Detail of the Thompson screen at the Green Howards' Chapel, 1931–32.

pigs and other fantastical creatures - remind us of Bromflet's carvings in Ripon. It is tempting to think that these images sowed seeds in the young Lewis Carroll's fervent imagination.

In the church, Thompson's work, completed between 1933 and 1945, dominates the Green Howards' Chapel, which commemorates members of the Regiment who died in the two world wars. Thompson's mice are found here on the screen (on the left hand post at the entrance to the chapel), on the chairs, altar rails, two altar stools (inscribed Scarborough and Beverley), a prie-dieu and chair. But the jewel in this particular treasury of Thompson work is the outstanding reredos. This bas-relief presents a 20th century interpretation of Calvary. Christ on the crucifix is transposed to a battle field scene from the second world war. Eight soldiers and two grave diggers prepare graves for the fallen against a background of blasted, bomb-damaged buildings. The piece is heart rending both in its juxtaposition of images and the skill and artistry of its execution.

From the church, it is just a short walk back to the market place and the Green Howards' regimental museum. Set in a converted 12th century church, the museum's collection spans the 300-year history of this famous regiment. The Thompson furniture here was originally produced for the officers' and sergeants' messes in the regiment's depot.

Robert Thompson's have close associations with other regiments. The Royal Signals, which has now moved from Catterick to Blandford in Dorset, has a large collection of Thompson furniture. A big central table to house a silver piece was made for the Prince of Wales Regiment. In 2008 a memorial settle for the Yorkshire Regiment was completed and placed on Darlington station platform, where it can be seen by all travellers.

Leaving Richmond, drive back towards St Mary the Virgin church and follow the signs for the A1 south towards Bedale. The route takes you in the direction of Easby Abbey. In fact, there is a pleasant riverside walk from Richmond Castle to Easby Abbey (a distance of about 5 miles). Visitors hoping to complete this full 'mouse tour' in one day are unlikely to have time to fit in this walk but it can be earmarked for a separate day. On the A1 travel south turning off on the A684 to Bedale.

Bedale

Bedale is one of Yorkshire's smallest market towns. The church of St Gregory at its centre dates back to an earlier Saxon church, which was given a north aisle towards the end of the 12th century and a south aisle a century later. The imposing tower is said to have been built as a refuge from border raiders.

From the grandeur of the Richmond reredos and the other regimental pieces, the Thompson work found in Bedale's St Gregory's church is refreshing in its small scale and simplicity. Here the mark of the mouse is found on a number of individual pieces including a credence table, octagonal table and some quite delightful children's stools. The choir stalls are also excellent examples of Thompson work.

Before leaving the church, take time to view the monuments. An alabaster knight, Sir Brian Fitzalan, Lord Lieutenant of Scotland, is shown with chain mail garb and flowing curls, his wife is by his side. Dating from the early 14th century, this is considered to be one of the finest examples of mediaeval sculpture in the country.

It is now just a short drive back to Ripon (on the B6268 and A6108), arriving in time to hear the horn blower at 9pm herald the close of the day.

11

THE LAKE DISTRICT (70 miles)

This seventy-mile round trip offers a busy one-day dash or a more leisurely weekend tour, through delightful countryside, with plenty of fine Mouseman pieces as highlights en route and many opportunities to take in the beauty spots of Lakeland.

Ambleside

The popular town of Ambleside at the north end of Windermere makes an excellent starting point for this scenic tour. Our first destination is Ambleside's Parish Church but on the way into town from the main car park, it's worth pausing for a quick look at a curious little building called Bridge House. Perched over Stock Ghyll, this tiny one-up, one-down former summer house was the home of a less illustrious woodworker – 'Chairy' Gill who lived there in the 1850s with his wife and six children.

At around the same time as the Gills were crammed into Bridge House, the Victorian architect George Gilbert Scott was busy with the construction of Ambleside's gothic Parish Church of St. Mary the Virgin (completed in 1854). To reach it: cross Stock Low Bridge, and then leave the bustle of the town centre behind, turning down Compston Road and then into Vicarage Road (by the cinema). Inside St Mary's Wordsworth Chapel is a modern 'mouse' piece: a panel on the east wall, commissioned in the 1980s by the church's curate, in memory of her mother.

Back in the car, head northeast out of Ambleside on an unclassified road signposted for Kirkstone. This road is also known as 'The Struggle' but is well worth the effort for its excellent views. Having met up with the A592, continue north through the Kirkstone pass - near the top there is an opportunity to pause and admire the views, as well as the delights of the Kirkstone Pass Inn (England's third highest pub). Carry on down the other side, past Brotherswater to Patterdale, our next Mouseman spot.

Patterdale

Surrounded by steep fells, the mid nineteenth century church of St Patrick is between Patterdale and Glenridding on the shores of Ullswater. On display in the church is a pair of staves with Thompson's distinctive fine-adzed finish. The staves are decorated in colour – one with the shamrock of St Patrick and the other with a Bishop's mitre. On the reverse of each is a shield with the legend 'E.A.H. 1955' and a mouse carved in bas relief. Both mice are complete with paws; on the Shamrock stave, the tail is curved under its body, whilst on the Mitre stave it dangles down over the shield.

Other features to look out for at the church are tapestry panels by Ann Macbeth (1875-1948) - a leading embroidress, who lived in Patterdale. One of them - 'The Nativity' - is loaned to the church each summer by the Glasgow Corporation. Another -

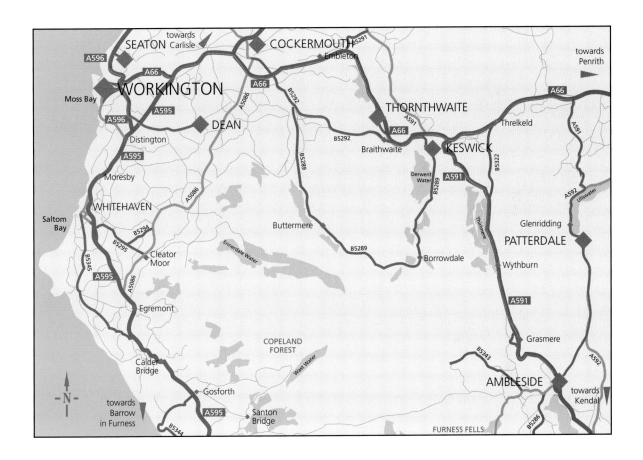

'The Good Shepherd' – depicts Christ as a shepherd, against a backdrop of Lakeland fells, including Hartsop, Deepdale, Caudale Moor and Kirkstone. The music to the hymn 'Jerusalem' is at the bottom of the tapestry and the story goes that Queen Mary liked it so much, that she burst into song when she saw it for the first time!

From Patterdale, carry on alongside Ullswater to the A5091 road that will take you towards Keswick, through Dockray and Matterdale End.

Before leaving Ullswater, it's worth making a quick detour on foot to the magnificent Aira Force waterfall, which offers a dramatic picnic spot and pleasant woodland stroll (National Trust car parks are by the lake and a short way up the Dockray road).

Take the A66 towards Keswick, where the shops and attractions of this busy market town offer a tempting place to stop off - especially if you have opted to spread this tour over more than one day.

Thornthwaite

The next destination is the church of St Mary, in the village of Thornthwaite. The village is located on a loop of unclassified road just off the A66 between Keswick and Bassenthwaite Lake. St Mary's church was originally built in the mid 1700s but then later remodelled in the early nineteenth century. Inside, mouse-seekers will immediately home in on the Bishop's chair, usually located beside the altar. Carved by Thompson, it is decorated with a coat of arms picked out in blue and the mouse is to be found scurrying along its top edge.

If you are keen on local arts and crafts, Thornthwaite Gallery is well worth a visit before leaving the village - it displays and sells works by local artists and during the summer months there are often craft demonstrations too.

Return by car back to the A66 and head west towards Seaton. Fans of Wordsworth may not be able to resist a brief detour to Cockermouth, to visit the birthplace of the ultimate romantic and Wordsworth House - the poet's childhood home. This has been restored by the National Trust and the house and gardens are opened at selected times from April to November.

Back on the Mouseman trail, carry on towards Workington. Two miles to the northeast is Seaton and the church of St Paul – our next destination.

Seaton

This small village church was built in 1883 by George Watson of Keswick and is a chapel of ease to the nearby church of St Peter, Camerton. The work here is more recent and includes choir stalls, two prie-dieux (kneeling prayer desks) and the pulpit. All the pieces were commissioned by the mother of John Fisher, who was Church Warden at St Paul's from 1951-1970; the book ledge on the south choir stalls carries a carved inscription in his memory.

Workington

On now, to one of the highlights of the tour - the collection of Thompson carved pieces at the town's Benedictine priory of Our Lady, Star of the Sea and St. Michael. To find the priory, go northwest up Workington High Street, which then becomes Guard Street. Turn left into Bank Street and continue into Banklands, where you will find the priory. It was built in 1876, with typically geometrical Victorian features on the outside but inside is a treasure trove of vintage and more modern Mouseman carving.

The early pieces include the choir stalls - pre-mouse - complete with a fascinating set of misericords that show scenes from Aesop's Fables. One of the bench ends has a scene depicting a donkey in a pulpit, a symbolic warning against listening to preaching fools and false teachers. Look out on the north (altar) side of the choir for a multi-purpose stand,

Opposite:
Top:
Windermere, arguably the best known of all the lakes. At its north end is Ambleside, where the parish church has modern 'mouse' work in its Wordsworth Chapel.

Bottom: Patterdale, seen from the descent from Kirkstone Pass. St Patrick's Church, with its distinctive pair of staves by Thompson, is between Patterdale and Glenridding.

Opposite:
Top:
The 1921 choir stalls at Workington priory hark back to Bromflet's work at Ripon, especially in their depiction of mythological beasts.

Right:
A kneeler for Workington Priory. Thompson's own description of the carvings was that they showed 'the devil chained and a suspicious character handcuffed'.

Left:
An unusual stand at Workington Priory produced in 1922 and photographed by Robert Thompson prior to installation. His caption states that it represents 'the four ages of man, or the four seasons'.

which is just the job for stowing away awkward ecclesiastical accessories, such as banners, processional crosses or candle snuffers.

The more recent 'mouse-work' has the characteristic raised mouse of the second generation of carvers and includes a lectern and three leaflet/magazine tables with nicely carved ends.

Before heading back inland, Workington Hall offers a quick historical detour – the house, originally built in 1379, was visited by Mary Queen of Scots, after she fled Scotland in 1568.

Dean

The last port of call is another feast of Thompson carving – the church of St Oswald in Dean.

Dean is about 10 miles to the south east, on the way from Workington to Loweswater. The church is a venerable, 800 year-old place of worship that was given a Kilburn makeover in the late sixties. There are apparantly 20 'mice' inside the church and it is quite a challenge to locate them all. From August 1967 through to April 1968, the Thompson carvers completely refurnished the chancel, designing its new layout and supplying choir stalls, the pulpit, two priests' stalls, a lectern, all the pews and front panel. Also look out for gargoyles - a rare breed in this part of the world - St Oswald's is one of only three churches in Cumbria to contain them. Also of interest is an ancient preaching cross in the graveyard, which dates back to the 12th Century or earlier and is believed to have been used by the monks at Calder Abbey.

To round off this Lakeland mouse-odyssey, make your way back across to Keswick - you can choose between the forested slopes of the Whinlatter Pass (B5292) or the dramatic screes and quarries of the winding Honister Pass (B5289). After a restorative tour of the tearooms, head south to Grasmere for Wordsworth's home, Dove Cottage and his final resting place in St Oswald's church yard, before arriving back at your start point in Ambleside.

12 YORK: THE MOUSE CITY

The ancient city of York offers such an array of history, architecture, pageant and other diversions that there is far too much to absorb in one day.

Following the trail of the mouse, gives a special focus to a visit to the city: for first-timers as well as those who have been many times and have trod the traditional tourist routes. During this visit, you will take in the city's crown jewel - the Minster - and also some hidden gems that the 'hurry-scurry' of many York tourist trails pass by.

If arriving by car, park in the car park off Marygate just west of Bootham Bar. Leaving the car park, you will emerge onto Marygate. Proceed left towards Bootham.

Passengers arriving by train, from the station, head towards the city over Lendal Bridge. Once you have crossed the bridge, take the steps down to the river bank and follow the river west, with the gardens on your right. At Marygate, turn right, passing the car park on your left.

St Olave's

Half way along Marygate on your right is St Olave's Church. The dim light makes mouse spotting here particularly difficult. However, the pews in the chapel on the south side of the chancel are unmistakably Thompson. Chunky and heavily adzed with unusual castellated moulding, they date from c1936. The mouse is found on the front of the kneelers.

From St Olave's, continue along Marygate by the side of the Abbey walls, which date from the 13th and 14th centuries. At Bootham, turn right, on through Bootham Bar, passing the art gallery on your right and proceed up to The Minster.

The Minster

York Minster presents an awe-inspiring setting for some of Thompson's finest work. During the period 1935 to 1956, the Dean and Chapter of the Minster commissioned a large body of internal decorative work from two distinguished architects, Sir Charles Peers and his successor, Sir Albert Edward Richardson, President of the Royal Academy.

The execution of these designs was entrusted to Robert Thompson, demonstrating how the Kilburn wood carver's reputation had reached the highest levels of architectural and ecclesiastical sensibilities.

The KOYLI Chapel

Entering the Minster through the main west doorway, you head for the chapel dedicated to The King's Own Light Infantry (or KOYLIs as they are popularly known). Here a glass-fronted bookcase (from 1947) and a roll of honour of soldiers killed in action, are unmistakably Robert Thompson's work.

Bishop Savage's Chantry

Moving on a short way down this aisle, the next Thompson creation is a hidden gem and something of a surprise. On the right, above the 16th

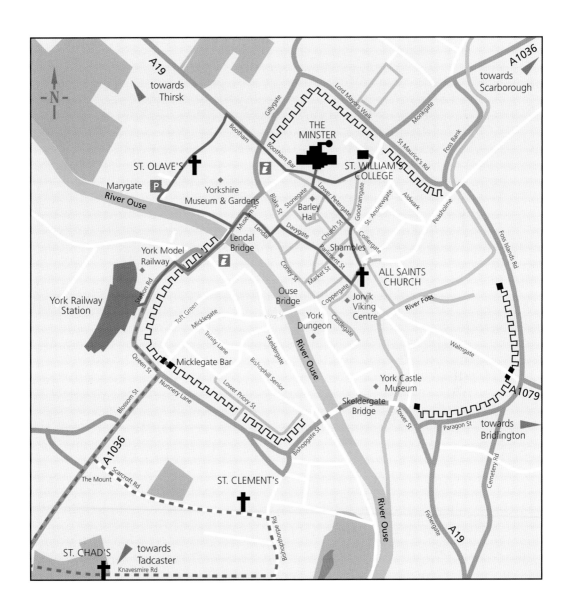

century tomb of Bishop Savage is a chantry designed by the architect Albert E Richardson. Completed by Robert Thompson in 1950, this small chapel on high is designed to accommodate two people and is accessed from the High Altar. Ornately carved wood with detail highlighted in gold and embroidered cloth at the sides, the Dean and Chapter of the cathedral praised Thompson 'for his brilliant execution of a design so different in character and detail from his customary work, it will stand as witness to posterity of our own generation's creative and executive ability, for we can show so few works of the standard of the past ages'.

St Stephen's Chapel
On to St Stephen's Chapel at the east end of the north choir aisle where

Thompson's mouse identifies the stall as his work. Completed in 1946, these pieces were the first he realised for architect, Albert Richardson.

Lady Chapel
Next to St Stephen's is the Lady Chapel. Eight oak seats are fitted into the stone screen behind which is the high altar. The prie-dieus are carved with delicate foliage and the mouse lurks on the side panels of the two outer prie-dieus and the central one. Thompson carried out this work in 1945 with lecterns for the chapel supplied the following year.

High Altar and Sanctuary
Turning now to the other side of the stone screen is the high altar and sanctuary. The Archbishop's chair here is a superb Thompson piece. On the north side of the sanctuary are five Deans' stalls with lace curtain effect tracery carved from the oak of the prie-dieus. Opposite these are three chairs and prie-dieus and servers' stalls. Whilst the rippled oak surfaces immediately identify these as

'Thompson', the enthusiast may be puzzled by the lack of the trademark mouse. In fact, Thompson was simply following strict instructions from the Dean who insisted that the altar should not be over-run with mice: no more than one mouse to every three stalls!

The Consistory Court
Before leaving the Minster, visitors should, if possible, seek access to the Consistory Court - special permission may be required. Here Thompson's work - the judge's seat and cupboard - is quite magnificent: the strong yet controlled carving and adzed ripples complement the sense of authority and tradition that is exuded by this small, enclosed court room.

To exit the Minster, leave by the south door. Immediately outside and to the right of the door take a look at the notice board. There is no mouse here and yet, although weather-beaten, the quality of the carving and the adzed finish are unmistakably Thompson's.

The Archbishop's chair, a superb piece on the high altar, was completed in 1949 and is dedicated to Bishop Woolcombe.

Opposite: Bishop Savage's Chantry, which was praised by the Dean and Chapter of the cathedral for its 'brilliant execution' of a design so different in character from Thompson's normal work. Completed in 1948, it features a plaque recording that it was paid for by the Terry family as a memorial to a son killed during the war.

REMEMBER
HARRY WOOLLCOMBE
FIRST SUFFRAGAN BISHOP OF WHITBY
1923 – 1939.

*Opposite:
All Saints
church in
Pavement has a
carved screen
with symbols
representing
Christ's Passion
and Crucifixion.
It was
completed in
1931.*

St William's College

Turning left now outside the south door and following the green round the east end of the Minster, leads into College Street. Founded in 1461, the college building offers a quiet courtyard behind heavy double doors studded with iron. It is these doors that attract our attention for a close examination of the right door shows the tell-tale mouse nestling within one of the upper panels. His partner on the left door has long since disappeared.

Having explored St William's Chapel (and perhaps enjoyed refreshments here) retrace your steps back to the south door of the Minster. Take the path opposite which is sign-posted to The Shambles, then turn left down Low Petergate. Note at this junction, on the corner of High Petergate, a figure of Minerva, goddess of wisdom. Carry on past Grape Lane and onto King's Square. Cross the Square, turning right into King's Court and then left into The Shambles.

The Shambles is one of the oldest streets in York. The name comes from 'shamel', meaning stalls or benches on which meat is displayed, a reference to the old butchers' quarter of the city. Today, the narrow street of The Shambles is invariably bustling with tourists and shoppers. Half way along the street, look out for the house of Margaret Clitheroe on the right. One of York's catholic martyrs, she met her death in 1586. Today her house is preserved as a simple shrine, largely overlooked by the tourist throng, it provides a welcome haven for quiet contemplation.

All Saints, Pavement

At the end of The Shambles, you emerge onto Pavement and turn right here. This was one of the first mediaeval streets to have a paved way. It was formerly the scene of public gatherings, including executions. On the left at the end of Pavement is Piccadilly, where a 'Mouseman' discovery was made when a former coffeeshop became a Wine Lodge. During the refurbishment, it was found that a carved timber frieze above the shop front had been painted over and then forgotten.

All Saints church lies straight ahead at the end of Pavement. In years gone by, a fire was lit every night in the lantern tower to guide travellers to York through the Forest of Galtres. Two massive organ-cases dominate with the mouse recessed on the right case. The work was carried out by Robert Thompson's successors in the early 1960s but the master's inspiration is clearly evident. In addition, two prieu-dieus are sited in front of the altar again with a recessed mouse on the right. The panels on the left and right of the reredos are finely crafted with symbols representing the passion and crucifixion of Christ.

Leaving the church, turn onto Parliament Street, a wide, paved thoroughfare which is usually home to various street performers. Carry on into Davygate, past Betty's famous tea rooms, look out for their own brand 'mouse bread' displayed in wooden bowls carved by the craftsmen in Kilburn. Proceed across St Helen's Square into Lendal and then left at Museum Street.

Follow the road down to the River Ouse. Carry on straight over Lendal

bridge to return to the train station.

To return to the car park, do not cross over Lendal Bridge, instead take the steps down to the river bank and then follow the path alongside the gardens on the right. This pleasant riverside walk eventually leads to Marygate. Turn right here and the car park is then on your left.

At this point, you may wish to conclude the tour but if time (and weary legs) allow, visits to St Chad's and St Clement's are highly recommended as they are home to some really beautiful pieces of Thompson work.

St Chad's

As this church is situated someway off the beaten track (approximately one mile outside the city centre) it is recommended to check in advance that access is available so that your visit is not in vain. Telephone 01904 654707.

From the city centre, head in the direction of the station and then follow Queen Street out to Micklegate Bar. This was traditionally the monarch's entrance into the city and was also the site upon which traitors' heads were displayed. From here, follow signs to the racecourse along Blossom Street and then The Mount. Just before the racecourse, turn left into Knavesmire Road. St Chad's, an unprepossessing red brick building is situated a short distance along on the left.

It is well worth the trip as inside, the pulpit is Thompson's work as are two leather seated chairs for the Bishop and Officiant, the font cover and two oak alms dishes.

St Clement's

To reach St. Clement's, carry on past St. Chad's until you meet Bishopthorpe Road, turn left and then second left into Scarcroft Road. The church is on your right.

The pieces here are early Thompson and are on a par with those found at Workington Priory. St. Clement's is considered to be home to some of Thompson's finest work. For opening times telephone: 01904 624 425.

Opposite: Pieces destined for St Clement's, York, photographed by Robert Thompson in his workshop in 1924.

13 NEAR AND FAR

Robert Thompson lived, worked and died in Kilburn but his work travelled far. A selection is described and illustrated in this chapter and the reference section at the end of this book provides a list of Thompson's commissions across the country.

London

It is appropriate that Robert Thompson's work should feature in Westminster Abbey.

Commissions for the Abbey are an accolade and demonstrate just how far Thompson's reputation had spread among leading architects and the great and the good.

Robert Thompson received such a commission in 1942 to provide two large standing altar candlesticks as a memorial to men who perished when HMS Barham was sunk in the Mediterranean the previous year. The candlesticks are unusual examples of Thompson work as the detail is picked out in blue, red and gold. Although there are other examples of coloured candlesticks, including some at Ripon Cathedral, Thompson did not favour the use of colour believing that the natural hue of the wood should be enough to carry the design of a piece.

The candlesticks were installed and dedicated at a memorial service in February 1943 and are decorated every year with a floral tribute at a memorial service organised by the survivors of HMS Barham. Following their installation, a second commission followed from the widow of the Barham's Commanding Officer,

Captain GC Cook, for a pair of two-foot candlesticks for the nave altar. Having received the commission on October 7th 1943, Robert Thompson made extra effort to deliver the work quickly. A postcard response confirms this, he wrote: 'I will do my best to have the Altar candlesticks completed for the date you mention, but really cannot promise to do so as I have a great deal of work in hand, and labour is very difficult these days. However, you know I will do my best.' And so he did, the candlesticks were delivered in less than seven weeks, in time for the memorial service on 25th November 1943.

Also in the Abbey is a credence table, dating from the same time as the candlesticks, it commemorates the wife of the Bishop of Chichester.

Robert Thompson's also has close links with two colleges in the London area. In the 1930s it supplied tables, benches, chairs and a pair of distinctive gong stands to Haileybury College, situated on the northern outskirts of the capital in Hertfordshire. Founded by the East India Company in 1806, it is now an independent co-educational boarding school and numbers among its old scholars such diverse names as Clement Atlee, Alan Ayckbourn, Rudyard Kipling, Stirling Moss and Lord Sainsbury.

The other college is Goodenough, the prestigious postgraduate institute in central London. Robert Thompson supplied no fewer that thirty-eight tables for its Great Hall in 1937, shortly after the college opened. After seventy years of use they were

Robert Thompson outside the Kilburn workshop with the credence table for Westminster Abbey.

showing distinct signs of wear and tear and so have recently been refurbished at Kilburn. Chris Wright, Warden of the college's London House, commented: "Being made of solid English oak the furniture is very heavy and the tables can be difficult to move. Our initial thought was to replace them with furniture that we could stack, but Robert Thompson's is a national institution and the tables are part of the fabric of our college, so refurbishment was the only option."

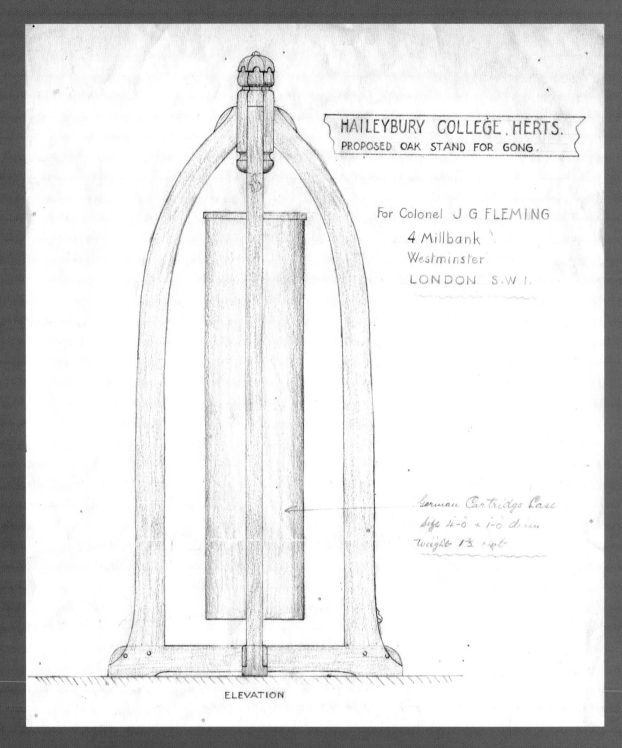

One of two memorial gong stands made for the refectory at Haileybury College in London. This one, based on a German shell case, was designed in 1931.

One of the Haileybury College gong stands is on the left of this photograph, which shows Robert Thompson in the centre of the group. The figure on the right is sitting in an early monk's chair.

ELEVATION

Detail of a drawing – with carefully executed graining – for a fireplace for Sir Peter Horlick. Robert Thompson supplied many tables, desks and chairs for the offices of the Horlick's drinks company in the London area, as well as items for the home of its proprietor.

Opposite:
Robert designed many fireplaces and their surrounds. The drawing for this one at Kepwick Hall, north of Thirsk, dates from 1933.

Proposed Fireplace to Schoolroom at
KEPWICK HALL

FRONT ELEVATION

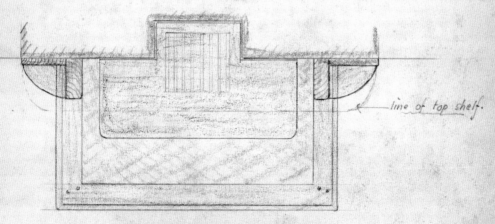

line of top shelf.

PLAN

Scale 1" — 1'

Opposite:
Top:
*These choir
stalls at Elmore
Abbey, near
Newbury were
completed in
1995.*

Bottom:
*Refectory table
for St Edmund's
College,
Cambridge,
recently
completed at
Kilburn.*

Elsewhere in England

Working outwards from London, a selection of places with Thompson associations begins with Elmore Abbey, the Anglican Benedictine monastery at Speen, near Newbury. Here seven choirs stalls, nave benches and sacristy furniture were completed in 1995. The abbey, with its wonderfully maintained cloistered garden, can be visited by prior arrangement. Phone 01635 33080.

Heading north to Cambridge, Robert Thompson was commissioned in the 1930s by St Edmund's College to make three refectory tables, each sixteen feet in length. Thirty years later came an order for an even longer 19ft table. A varied array of work in recent years has included a new altar for the chapel, a large cabinet to house the college silver, a pair of Vice Master's chairs and three more tables. Founded in 1896, St Edmund's is unique among Cambridge University colleges in following the Roman Catholic rather than the Anglican tradition.

Continuing north through the rolling countryside of Lincolnshire ultimately leads to the tiny village of Alkborough, close to both the Humber estuary and the lower reaches of the River Trent. Its parish church is unremarkable except for the fact that it provides one of the few instances where both a drawing and a photograph of Thompson work in the 1920s can be compared.

To the south-west at Retford is Ranby House, a Woodard School that has its own 'Mouse' dormitory as well as other pieces of vintage Thompson furniture. Another school with strong 'mouse' associations is Leeds Girls' High, where one former pupil certainly impressed her eight-year-old daughter.

She described to her how the library had been fitted out by Robert Thompson and that the mice were everywhere, adding that she and her friends would look to see if they were under the shelves or round the back. The daughter later wrote: "In my imagination I thought the carved mice actually moved, in some magical way, and assumed the shelves were honeycombed with tiny tunnels, from which they would pop out or vanish into if startled!"

The many examples of 'Mouse" work in Leeds churches include desks, frontals and kneelers as well as an attractive screen at St Michael's in Headingley. They were completed about 1938.

Apart from York and the various 'trails' featured earlier in this book, it is also worth heading further north towards the Tyne, pausing at Sunderland where two Roman Catholic churches have Thompson fixtures and fittings of special interest that have been installed from 1998 onwards. Items at the Holy Rosary in Farringdon include a tabernacle, lectern, presidential chair and three solid oak doors. Carvings depict the local coal mine's pit head, while an adzed finish to the altar is a reminder of the nearby River Wear and the area's shipbuilding heritage. Work at the nearby Immaculate Heart of Mary, in Springwell, ranges from a crucifix and tabernacle plinth to a side credence shelf and a sanctuary lamp holder.

There is also much to see in the cathedral city of Durham. Apart from a sanctuary chair in the magnificent cathedral itself, it is also worth seeking out the fine collections of Mouseman furniture at St Giles church and St Mary Magdalene, Belmont, as well as

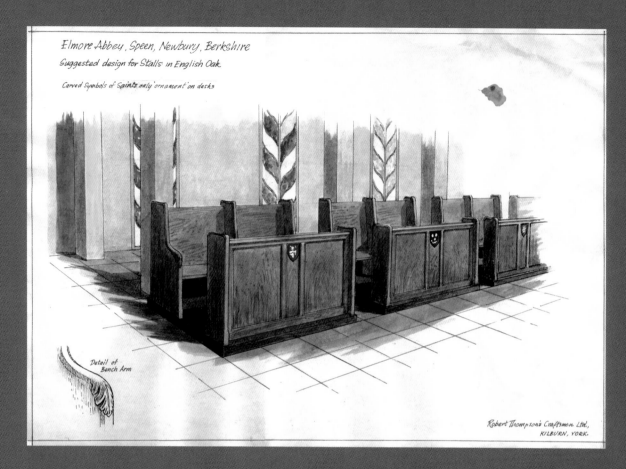

Elmore Abbey, Speen, Newbury, Berkshire
Suggested design for Stalls in English Oak.

Carved Symbols of Saints only 'ornament' on desks

Detail of
Bench Arm

Robert Thompson's Craftsmen Ltd.,
KILBURN, YORK.

Both the
original
drawing and
an early
photograph of
the 1922
reredos at
Alkborough
parish church
in Lincolnshire
have survived,
thus providing
a rare insight
into how
design changes
were
sometimes
made as work
evolved. The
pierced central
tracery was
simplified and
the panels
either side
reduced from
three to two,
while the
proposed
inscription
along the top
was omited.

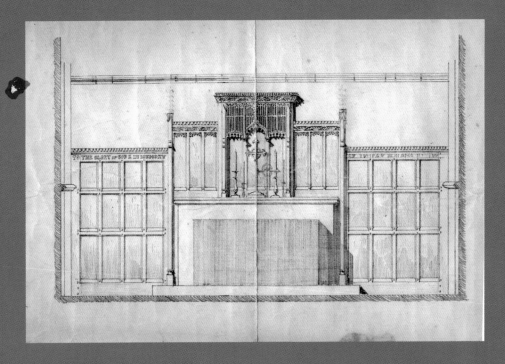

Screen at St Michael's church in Headingley, Leeds, with pierced tracery at the top contrasting with the very simple adzed panels. Completed in 1938, it created a children's corner that could separate Sunday School activities from the rest of the church.

Opposite:
The 1959 screen at Brecon Cathedral, a continuation of the mediaeval tradition that inspired Thompson. The pierced tracery and carved shields are especially noteworthy. The broken moulding across the top is a feature closely associated with the architect A D R Caroe.

St Mary's College. Other recommended locations in County Durham include St Aidan Colliery Church at Annfield Plain, Coxhoe parish church, the Duke of York Inn at Fir Tree and the Blue Bell Inn at Stanley.

Wales

Robert Thompson's work is to be found in many parts of Wales. The 'vast collection' in Bangor Cathedral was started in 1954, just before his death the following year, and was completed in 1960. The earliest piece is the screen at the east end of the north aisle in the north transept. A second screen in the south aisle followed in 1960, and there is also a fine font cover from the Kilburn workshop.

Further west is St Benedict's church at Gryffin, Conway, with its noteworthy choir stalls and pulpit.

At the opposite end of Wales is Brecon Cathedral, where work was completed after Thompson's death – it was dedicated by the Bishop of Swansea and Brecon in 1963. It clearly demonstrates the continuance of his ideas and the inspiration he found in the work of mediaeval craftsmen. The magnificent oak screen in the Cordwainers chapel was commissioned by the London architect A D R Caroe (a firm with which Robert Thompson had forged a strong working relationship). The piece was commissioned as a continuation of a mediaeval screen, which runs along one side of the chapel. The Kilburn screen comprises two panels, one of which depicts a goat's head, the Cordwainers traditional emblem. The other panel shows the tools of the shoemakers' and leather workers' trade. The screen is topped with fine tracery with the 'mouse' appearing at the foot of the far right column.

When in South Wales, it is also worth visiting St Woolos Cathedral at Newport with its many Thompson fittings. St Martin's church at Caerphilly has a large collection, and also recommended are St Margaret's at Mountain Ash and St Peter's at Fairwater, Cardiff.

It is difficult to resist the temptation to continue further west, where St Martin's at Haverfordwest has much of interest. Its location is eclipsed by the exquisitely sited St David's Cathedral, which also has a large collection of Thompson work.

Scotland

As might be expected, Thompson work in Scotland is extremely scattered. The Benedictine Priory at Pluscarden, near Elgin in Moray, has some superb examples in the form of the misericords on the choir stalls. These are in the chancel of the Abbey Church, which dates back to 1260. Whilst the Church is open 365 days a year, visits to the chancel are only by prior arrangement, upon which one of the monks will be happy to show Thompson's work. To make arrangements, telephone 01343 890257.

Across the broad Moray Firth is Dornoch, with its modern Celtic cross in the 'cathedral of the Highlands'.

For sheer remoteness, it is difficult to equal the small Hebridean island of Canna immediately to the west of Rum. Its few buildings include the Roman Catholic church of St Edward built by a former Marquis of Bute. Inside the church, the oak communion rail, complete with 'mouse' was originally donated to Glenforsa Chapel by the Beale family of Glenforsa. When the chapel closed, it was taken to Canna, arriving there about 1953.

Further afield

Thompson's work reaches the furthest corners of the earth. Known pieces include a 'wheel' for Stavanger Inner Wheel in Norway, a font cover for the Deanery at Nassau in the Bahamas, a kneeler for the Bishop of Gambia and a whole array of items for Grahamstown Cathedral in South Africa. There have also been speaker's chairs for parliaments in locations as diverse as Nepal, the Solomon Islands and Tonga. The 'mouse' has indeed travelled far – from Kilburn to Katmandu!

Speaker's Chair for the Nepalese Parliament, delivered in 1992.

Opposite: Some Thompson furniture has even gone to sea! Tony Wedgwood-Benn stands in the centre of this photograph of two chairs made for the Ark Royal in 1954. It is thought they were for use in the ship's chapel.

Octagonal pulpit at Berkswell parish church, Warwickshire, photographed in Kilburn when completed in 1927.

ROBERT THOMPSON'S WORK Compiled by Christopher Scaife, Kilburn

The following gazetteer is currently the most comprehensive guide to work completed by Robert Thompson and his successors. The list shows sites of the 'mouse' in churches, boardrooms, schools, inns & etc. and is constructed from the incomplete archive records of Robert Thompson's Craftsmen Ltd. (The areas used are not necessarily today's county boundaries.)

Place	Area	Site	Description	Earliest Date
Abbots Langley	Herts	St.Lawrence Bedmond	Few	1998
Aberdeen	Scot.N	Art/Industrial Museum	Benches	1954
Aberdeen	Scot.N	Marischal College	Furniture	1948
Aberford	Yorks.W	St.Ricarius	Several	1941
Abingdon	Oxon	Denman Col. for Crafts	Furniture	
Accrington	Lancs	St.Andrew	Several	1961
Accrington	Lancs	St.Augustine	Font	2001
Ackworth	Yorks.S	St.Cuthbert	Stall	1962
Acomb	York	Baptist Ch	Few	1968
Acomb	York	Holy Redeemer	Large	1933
Acomb	York	Methodist	Missal Stand	1947
Acomb	York	St.Aidan	Several	1937
Adare	Eire	Adare Ch	Screen	1948
Addingham	Yorks.S	St.Peter	Several	1938
Adel	Yorks.W	St.John	Several	1953
Ainderby Steeple	Yorks.N	St.Helen	Few	1948
Ainsdale	Lancs	St.John	Several	1961
Castleford	Yorks.W	Holy Cross Airedale	Large	1934
Akeley Wood	Bucks	Shirley House School	Few	1940
Aldborough	Yorks.N	St.Paul	Several	1932
Alderbury	Wilts	St.Mary	CredTable	1968
Aldershot	Hants	St.George	Screens	1960
Alkborough	Lincs	St.John-t-B	Few	1922
Allesley	Warks	All Saints	Seating	1977
Almondbury	Yorks.W	St.Michael & St.Helen	Several	1948
Alne	Yorks.N	Cheshire Home Alne Hall	Table	1959
Alne	Yorks.N	St.Mary	Several	1938
Althorp	Nhants	Althorp Park	Several	1936
Altofts	Yorks.W	St.Mary	CredTable	1983
Alton	Hants	All Saints	Board	1999
Alton	Hants	Four Monks	MemTable	1964
Altrincham	Ches	St.Margaret	Several	1961
Ambleside	Cumbria	Charlotte Mason College	Furniture	1930
Ambleside	Cumbria	St.Mary	Board	1986
Amcotts	Lincs	Ch	Lectern	1963
Amotherby	Yorks.N	St.Helen	Few	1947
Ampleforth	Yorks.N	Abbey Ch	Very large	1922
Ampleforth	Yorks.N	College	Very large	1921
Ampleforth	Yorks.N	Village RC Ch	Several	1919
Angmering-on-Sea	Sussex	Ch	Lectern	1967
Anlaby	Yorks.E	St.Peter	Few	1938
Annfield Plain	Durham	St.Johns Meth. Ch.	Several	1940
Appleton Wiske	Yorks.N	St.Mary	Few	1953
Appletreewick	Yorks.N	St.John-t-B	Several	1945
Arkengarthdale	Yorks.N	St.Mary	Few	1946
Armley	Yorks.W	Ch	Plates	1953
Ascot	Berks	St.Marys School	Board	2004
Ashington	NLand	Holy Sepulcre	Few	1966
Ashington	NLand	PChurch Mothers Union	Few	1971
Ashover	Derby	Rectory	Few	1963
Askham Bryan	York	St.Nicholas	Stand	1965
Askrigg	Yorks.N	Weatherald Ltd	Boardroom	1996
Askrigg	Yorks.N	Yorebridge Gram.Sch.	Few	1954
Athersley	Yorks.S	St.Helen	Pedestal	1980
Attercliffe	Yorks.S	Ch	Grave Board	1936
Aycliffe	Durham	Ch	Few	1970
Aysgarth	Yorks.N	Aysgarth School	Several	1956
Babworth	Notts	All Saints	Few	1958
Baildon	Yorks.W	St.John the Evangelist	Candlestick	1995
Bainton	Yorks.E	St.Andrew	Several	1948
Bakewell	Derby	All Saints	Few	
Balkwell	NLand	St.Peter	Several	1938
Bamber Bridge	Lancs	St.Mary	Crucifix	1921
Bamford	Lancs	Congregational Ch	Chairs	1971
Bamford	Derby	United Reform Ch	Few	
Banff	Canada	Luxton Museum	Table	
Bangor	Wales	Cathedral	Large	1954
Bangor	Wales	Holy Trinity	Few	1962
Bardsey	Yorks.W	Ch	Several	1953
Barham	Kent	Barham Village	Board	1955
Barkisland	Yorks.W	Christchurch	Altar	2004
Barnard Castle	Durham	Barnard Castle School	Few	1965
Barnard Castle	Durham	Rotary Club	Wheel	1958
Barnard Castle	Durham	St.Mary	Several	1937
Barnard Castle	Durham	Trinity Methodist Ch	Case	1970
Barnsley	Yorks.S	Broadway Tech.G Sch.	Board	1962
Barnsley	Yorks.S	High School	Platform Set	1953
Barnsley	Yorks.S	Methodist Pitt St.	Several	1964
Barnsley	Yorks.S	St.George	Few	1965
Barnsley	Yorks.S	St.Paul	Chairs	1964
Barnsley	Yorks.S	St.Peter	Several	1944
Barnsley	Yorks.S	Wentworth Castle Coll.	Few	1961
Barrow-in-Furnace	Lancs	St.Paul	Several	1961
Barrow-on-Soar	Leics	Holy Trinity	Several	1961
Barry	Wales	All Saints	Candle sticks	1985
Barton	Yorks.N	Vicarage	Few	1987
Barton Seagrave	Nhants	Vicarage	Plates	1958
Barton Stacey	Hants	Ch	Cross	1937
Barton-le-Willows	Yorks.E	Blacksmiths Arms	Stools	1966
Barwick in Elmet	Yorks.W	All Saints	Few	1938
Bath	Somset	Argyle United Reform Ch	Missal	1980
Bath	Somset	Royal Photographic Soc.	Chairs	1984
Batley	Yorks.W	All Saints	Desk	1961
Batley	Yorks.W	Girls Grammar School	Platform Set	1954
Batley	Yorks.W	St.Luke	Reredos	1951
Batley	Yorks.W	St.Thomas	Altar	1955
Batley Carr	Yorks.W	Holy Trinity	Large	1932
Bawtry	Yorks.S	Waddington Shop	Fittings	1965
Beckwithshaw	Yorks.N	St.Michael & All Angels	Few	1948
Bedale	Yorks.N	Herdwise Ltd	Boardroom	
Bedale	Yorks.N	St.Gregory	Several	1946
Bedlington	NLand	Grammar School	Few	1970
Beeston	Yorks.W	St.Lukes Beeston Hill	Panelling	1953
Beeston	Yorks.W	St.Mary	Several	1950
Belfast	NI	Kings Street Ch	Few	1955
Belmont	Durham	St.Mary Mag.	Several	1950
Ben Rhydding	Yorks.W	Methodists	Cross	1964
Ben Rhydding	Yorks.W	St.John the Evangelist	Several	1950
Benfieldside	Durham	St.Cuthbert	CredTable	1937
Bentham	Cumbria	St.John the Baptist	Board	1962
Berkeley	Glos	St.Mary	Several	1948
Berkswell	Warks	St.John-the-Baptist	Large	1927

Place	Area	Site	Description	Earliest Date
Berwick-o-Tweed	NLand	Castle Hotel	Several	1951
Berwick-o-Tweed	NLand	St.Cuthbert	Xstool	1964
Beverley	Yorks.E	Minster	Large	1948
Beverley	Yorks.E	St.Mary	Door	1955
Beverley	Yorks.E	St.Nicholas	Altar	1953
Bewdley	Worcs	Ch	Lectern	1994
BFPOR	Germany	4thArmour Brig.HQ	Few	1970
Bideford	Devon	Ch	Seating	
Bierley	Yorks.W	St.John the Evangelist	CredTable	1997
Billingham	Tees	St.Cuthbert	Several	1937
Billingham	Tees	Wynyard Training College	Missal stands	1958
Bilsdale	Yorks.N	St.Hilda	Plaque	1967
Bilsdale Midcable	Yorks.N	St.John	Several	1936
Bingham	Notts	St.Mary & All Saints	Large	1956
Bingley	Yorks.W	Ch	Altar rails	1962
Bingley	Yorks.W	Grammar School	Platform set	1958
Birchencliffe	Yorks.W	St.Philip	Font Cover	1949
Bircle	Lancs	St.John	Chairs	1950
Birdsall	Yorks.N	St.Mary	Cross	1936
Birkenhead	Ches	Christchurch	Font	1967
Birkenhead	Ches	High School	Desk	1966
Birmingham	Warks	RC Cathedral	Desk	1929
Birstall	Yorks.W	St.Peter	Several	1949
Birtswith	Yorks.N	St.James	Several	1950
Bishop Auckland	Durham	St.Helen	Candlesticks	1945
Bishop Auckland	Durham	St.Peter	Crucifix	1969
Bishop Burton	Yorks.E	All Saints	Panelling	1964
Bishop Sutton	Somset	St.Nicholas	Several	1969
Bishop Thornton	Yorks.N	St.Joseph	Candlesticks	1957
Bishop Wearmouth	Durham	St.Nicholas	Font	
Bishops Sutton	Hants	St.Nicholas	Several	1969
Bishopthorpe	York	St.Andrew	Several	1921
Bishopton	Tees	Ch	Staves	1949
Blackburn	Lancs	Well Ch	Tablet	1937
Blackhall	Durham	St.Andrew	Several	1945
Blackpool	Lancs	Ch	Stall	1964
Blackpool	Lancs	Holy Cross	Large	1954
Blackpool	Lancs	Royal Oak Hotel	Panelling	1930
Blackpool	Lancs	St.Paul	Large	1937
Blacktoft,Goole	Yorks.E	Holy Trinity	Several	1950
Blandford Forum	Dorset	Royal Signals HQ Mess	Plaques	1997
Blaydon	Tyne	Ch	Chair	1954
Bleadon	Somset	Ch	Cred.Table	
Boldon West	Durham	Ch	Font Cover	1972
Boltby	Yorks.N	Hesketh Inn	Bar	1969
Boltby	Yorks.N	Holy Trinity	Several	1946
Bolton	Lancs	Canon Slade Gram. Sch.	Platform Set	
Bolton	Lancs	Ch	Stand	1996
Bolton	Lancs	Humoni Ch	Few	1954
Bolton Abbey	Yorks.N	St.Mary & Cuthbert	Several	1937
Bolton Percy	Yorks.W	All Saints	Several	1928
Bolton,Bradford	Yorks.W	St.James	Few	1958
Bolton-le-Sands	Lancs	United Ref.	Several	1965
Bolton-on-Swale	Yorks.N	St.Mary	Few	1935
Boosebeck	Yorks.N	St.Aidan	Lectern	1961
Boroughbridge	Yorks.N	Langthorpe	Mem.Board	1959
Borrowby	Yorks.N	Chapel	Tablet	1958
Bossall	Yorks.N	St.Botolf	Several	1966
Boston	Lincs		Mem.Tablet	1950
Boston Spa	Yorks.W	St.Mary	Few	1938
Bournemouth	Hants	Annunciation Ch	Pulpit	1964
Bowburn	Durham	Christ the King	Several	1948
Bowdon	Ches	St.Margaret	Font Cover	
Bowness-o-Solway	Cumbria	Ch	Prayer Desk	1956
Bracewell	Yorks.N	St.Michael	Seating	1968
Bradford	Yorks.W	Belle Vue Girls High Sch	Several	1949
Bradford	Yorks.W	Bradford Golf Club	Several	1932
Bradford	Yorks.W	Catholic Landsdown Place	Reredos	
Bradford	Yorks.W	City Hall	Chair	1970
Bradford	Yorks.W	Civic Society	Memorial	1969
Bradford	Yorks.W	Girls Grammar School	Library	1936
Bradford	Yorks.W	Gratten Offices	Large	1930
Bradford	Yorks.W	Holme Lane Cong. Ch	Several	1957
Bradford	Yorks.W	St.Cuthbert	Few	1962
Bradford	Yorks.W	St.James Bolton Road	Stall	
Bradford	Yorks.W	St.John Broadway	Stall	
Braeburn	Cumbria	churchyard	Crosses	1943
Brafferton	Yorks.N	St.Peter	Few	1961
Braithwell	Yorks.S	All Hallows	Few	1950
Bramhope	Yorks.W	St.Giles	Several	1942
Bramshott	Hants	Parish Ch	Several	
Bramwith	Yorks.S	Bramwith Hall	Few	1942
Brancepath	Durham	St.Brandon	Few	1967
Brandon	Suffolk	Rectory	Few	1963
Bransby	Yorks.N	All Saints	Several	1913
Brantingham	Yorks.E	Parish Ch	Headstones	1945
Branxton	NLand	St.Paul	Altar	1958
Brassington	Derby	Ch	Bookcase	1964
Braunton	Devon	St.Brannocks	Pews	1958
Brecon	Wales	Cathedral	Large	1960
Brentford	Midsex	St.John	Chairs	1958
Brentwood	Essex	Ursuline Convent	Seating	1967
Bridgewater	Somset	Holy Trinity	large	1960
Bridlington	Yorks.E	Christ Ch	Several	1941
Bridlington	Yorks.E	Greatham Hospital	Chair	1962
Bridlington	Yorks.E	High School for Girls	Chairs	1965
Bridlington	Yorks.E	Hospital Mortuary Chapel	Several	1966
Bridlington	Yorks.E	Lords Feoffer	Several	1934
Bridlington	Yorks.E	Priory	Very large	1919
Brighouse	Yorks.W	St.Chad	Memorial	
Brighouse	Yorks.W	St.Joseph RC Presbyt.	Few	1961
Brighouse	Yorks.W	St.John Clifton	Few	1967
Brinklow	Warks	St.John t B	Rail	1970
Bristol	Somset	3 Kings of Cologne	Few	1965
Bristol	Somset	Barstaple House Chapel	Several	1980
Bristol	Somset	Bristol Grammar School	Missal stand	1997
Broadway	Worcs	Ch	Lectern	1988
Brodsworth	Yorks.S	Ch	Lectern	1943
Bromley	Kent	Ch	Platform Set	1986
Bromley	Kent	St.Joseph RC	Seating	1964
Brompton	Yorks.N	St.Thomas	Few	1949
Bromsgrove	Worcs	Hospital Chapel	Lectern	1954
Brotherton	Yorks.W	Ch	Few	1961
Brotton	Yorks.N	St.Margaret	Few	1932
Brough	Yorks.E	Elloughton Ch	Few	1948
Bruntcliffe	Yorks.W	School	Few	1969
Bruntcliffe	Yorks.W	St.Andrew	Several	1949
Bubwith	Yorks.E	All Saints	Several	1943
Bucknell	Shrop	Ch.	Mem.Board	1932
Bulmer	Yorks.N	St.Martin	CredTable	1956
Bulwell	Notts	St.Mary	Several	1955
Buntingford	Herts	St.Richard of Chichester	Plaque	2005
Burghill	Heref	St.Mary	Stand	
Burkinshaw	Yorks.W	Ch	Reredos	
Burley	Hants	Ch	Table	1987
Burley-i-Wharfedale	Yorks.W	St.Mary	Large	1952
Burnhope	Yorks.W	Park Methodist Ch	Chair	1983
Burnley	Lancs	Ch	Tracery	2000
Burnley	Lancs	Masonic Hall	Seats	1955
Burnley	Lancs	St.Mary	Screen	1954
Burton Agnes	Yorks.E	St.Martin	Several	1951
Burton Leonard	Yorks.N	Hare and Hounds Inn	Few	1967
Burton Salmon	Yorks.W	Churchyard	War Mem.	1925
Bury St.Edmunds	Suffolk	Registry	Case	1964
Burythorpe	Yorks.E	All Saints	Few	1963
Buttercrambe	Yorks.E	St.John the Evangelist	Altar	1930
Byne	S.Africa	Ch	Alms Dish	
Caerphilly	Wales	St.Martin	Several	1956

Place	Area	Site	Description	Earliest Date
Calgary	Canada	Alta Ch	Font	1955
Cambridge	Cambs	Downing College	Candletick	1988
Cambridge	Cambs	Emmanuel College	Bookrest	1937
Cambridge	Cambs	Perse School for Girls	Chairs	1977
Cambridge	Cambs	Queen's College	Chest	1938
Cambridge	Cambs	St.Edmund College	Large	1940
Cambridge	Cambs	Trinity Hall	Kneelers	
Canna,Mull	Scot.N	St.Edward(from Glenforsa)	Altar rail	early
Canterbury	Kent	St.Augustine	Statue	1969
Carham	Scot.S	St.Cuthbert	Few	
Carleton,Leyburn	Yorks.W	Ch	Tablets	1963
Carleton-in-Craven	Yorks.W	St.Mary	Seating	1948
Carlin How	Yorks.N	Ch	Altar	
Carlton Husthwaite	Yorks.N	Manor House	Few	1928
Carlton Miniott	Yorks.N	St.Laurence	Few	1935
Carlton Towers	Lincs	Ch	Few	1950
Carlton-in-Cleveland	Yorks.N	Outdoor Centre	Missal stand	1982
Carlton-in-Cleveland	Yorks.N	St.Botolph	Few	1956
Carlton-on-Trent	Notts	Ch	Candlestick	1996
Carnforth	Lancs	Christchurch	Chairs	1968
Carperby	Yorks.N	Ch	Tablet	1955
Carsdon	Tyne	Ch	Hymn Board	1965
Castle Combe	Wilts	Manor House Hotel	Several	1967
Castle Craig	Scot.S	Chapel	Several	1996
Castle Eden	Durham	Brewery Boardroom	Furniture	1952
Castleford	Yorks.W	High School	Lectern	1972
Castleford	Yorks.W	Town Hall Chamber	Several	1958
Castleton	Lancs	St.Martin	Few	1964
Castleton	Yorks.N	St.Michael & St,George	Several	1935
Castleton,Thurso	Scot.N	St.Clair Arms Hotel	Chairs	
Catterick	Yorks.N	Colburn Lodge	Several	1947
Catterick	Yorks.N	Officer's Mess	Large	1936
Catterick	Yorks.N	Royal Airforce	Few	1942
Catterick	Yorks.N	Royal Anglian Regiment	Few	1969
Catterick	Yorks.N	Royal Engineers	Napkin Rack	1943
Catterick	Yorks.N	Royal Signals	Several	1939
Catterick	Yorks.N	Royal Tank 1st Regiment	Few	1968
Catterick	Yorks.N	St.Aidan Reg.Ch	Several	1947
Catterick	Yorks.N	St.Martin Garrison Ch	Few	1944
Catterick	Yorks.N	Vimmy Barracks Mess	Board	1988
Catterick Bridge	Yorks.N	Catterick Bridge Hotel	Fittings	1929
Catterick Old	Yorks.N	St.Anne	Several	1937
Cayton	Yorks.N	Methodist	Cross	1968
Cayton	Yorks.N	St.John-t-Baptist	Chair	1999
Chapel Allerton	Yorks.W	Ch	Plaque	1959
Chaplethorpe	Yorks.W	St.James	Few	1962
Charlecombe Bath	Somset	St.Mary	Seating	1967
Cheadle	Ches	Ch	Board	1982
Cheddington	Herts	Ch	Reredos	
Chelmsford	Essex	Ch	Alms Dish	1983
Chester	Ches	Cathedral	Few	1946
Chester	Ches	Queens School	Furniture	1954
Chester-le-Street	Durham	Cemetery Chapel	Several	1965
Chichester	Sussex	Cathedral	Few	1987
Chirton Moor	Durham	Ch	Porch	1957
Chipping Ongar	Essex	Ch	Stand	1951
Chop Gate	Yorks.N	Ch	Several	1939
Chorley	Lancs	Washington Hall Tra.Col.	Several	1949
Church Fenton	Yorks.W	St.Mary	Candlestick	
Cleadon	Durham	Ch	Gates	1954
Cleckheaton	Yorks.W	Central Methodist Chapel	Several	1952
Cleckheaton	Yorks.W	St.John	Several	1960
Clitheroe	Lancs	Waddow Hall(G.Guides)	Few	
Coalville	Leics	Abbey	Missal stand	
Cobham	Surrey	Ch	Dishes	1970
Cobham	Surrey	Sandroyd School	Several	1930
Cockerton	Tees	St.Mary	Few	1954
Cockfield	Durham	Churchyard (in Stone)	War Mem.	1922
Cockleford	Glos	Green Dragon Inn	Large	1997

Place	Area	Site	Description	Earliest Date
Codsall	Staffs	St.Nicholas	Chair	1937
Coedpoeth	Wales	St.Tudfil	Chair	1940
Colchester,Romon	Essex	1st Staffs.Reg.	Rack	1983
Colchester	Essex	Green Howards Ch	Plaque	1970
Coleman's Hatch	Sussex	Holy Trinity	Plaque	
Colinton	Scot.C	St.Cuthbert	Altar rails	
Collierley	Durham	St.Thomas	Several	1941
Collingham	Yorks.W	Ch	Few	1957
Colne	Lancs	Holy Trinity	Several	1950
Colwinston	Wales	St.Michael & All Angels	Few	1955
Colwyn Bay	Wales	Eglwysbach	Plaque	1999
Congresbury	Somset	St.Andrew	Dishes	1956
Conisbrough	Yorks.S	St.Peter	Pews	1962
Coniscliffe	Tees	St.Edwin	Lit.Table	1961
Coniston	Cumbria	St.Andrew	Pews	1957
Coniston Cold	Yorks.N	St.Peter	Chairs	2003
Conistone	Yorks.N	St.Mary	Several	1957
Constable Burton	Yorks.N	Ch	Altat rails	1963
Conway	Wales	St.Mary	Several	1959
Conway	Wales	Gyffin St.Benedicts	Several	1954
Coopersale, Epping	Essex	St.Alban	Pulpit	1950
Copmanthorpe	York	St.Giles	Chairs	1936
Corby	Cumbria	Corby Castle	Few	1937
Cornhill-on-Tweed	NLand	St.Helen	Few	1958
Cottingham	Yorks.E	St.Mary	Several	1961
Coventry	Warks	Cathedral	Chair	1943
Coventry	Warks	Stoke Park School	Lectern	1981
Coverham	Yorks.N	Ch	Few	1944
Cowling	Lancs	Ch	Stalls	1957
Cowpit	Lincs	St.Mary	Pulpit	1943
Coxhoe	Durham	St.Mary	Large	1944
Coxwold	Yorks.N	Fauconberg Arms	Several	1968
Coxwold	Yorks.N	St.Michael	Several	1923
Crambe	Yorks.E	St.Michael	Few	1943
Cramlington	Nland	St.Nicholas	Table	1999
Crathes Castle	Scot.N	Chapel	Stool	
Crayke	Yorks.N	St.Cuthbert	Cred.Table	1948
Crichton	Scot.C	Parish	Font	
Crickhowell	Wales	Gliffaes Country Hotel	Few	1987
Crocketford	Scot.S	Whitehill Ch	Pulpit	1958
Croft	Tees	Croft Autodrome	Bar	1967
Croft	Tees	Croft Spa Hotel	Several	
Crook	Durham	St.Catherine	Several	1947
Croxdale	Durham	Hall	Figure	1966
Croxdale	Durham	St.Bartholomew	Several	1957
Croydon South	Surrey	St.Pauls Presb.Ch	Table	1964
Cudworth	Yorks.S	St.John-t-Baptist	Candlesticks	1959
Cullercoats	Tyne	St.George	Mem.Seat	1969
Cundall	Yorks.N	Cundall Manor School	Library	1984
Cundall	Yorks.N	St.Mary & All Saints	Gates	1983
Dacre	Yorks.N	Holy Trinity	Several	1943
Dalby	Yorks.N	St.Peter	Rails	1930
Dalton	Yorks.N	Ch	Gates	1937
Dalton	Yorks.N	Royal Canadian Airforce	Bar Fittings	1944
Dalton-le-Dale	Durham	Ch	Few	1967
Danby	Yorks.N	St.Hilda	Several	1925
Danby Wiske	Yorks.N	Ch	Several	1943
Darley	Yorks.N	Ch	Dishes	1967
Darlington	Tees	Ch	CredTable	1954
Darlington	Tees	Ch	Reredos	1960
Darlington	Tees	Darlington Training College	Several	1953
Darlington	Tees	Eastbourne G Sec.Mod.Sch	Few	1957
Darlington	Tees	Fleece Hotel	Bar	1951
Darlington	Tees	Holy Trinity	Several	1959
Darlington	Tees	St.Cuthbert	Several	1947
Darlington	Tees	St.John	Lectern	1961
Darlington	Tees	St.Mark	Altar	
Darlington	Tees	Vicarage	CredTable	1953
Darrington	Yorks.W	St.Luke & All Saints	Several	1948

Place	Area	Site	Description	Earliest Date
Dawdon	Durham	St. Helen	Several	1962
Dawnham	Lancs	Ch	Altar	1973
Dean	Cumbria	St.Oswald	Large	1967
Dearnley	Lancs	St.Andrew Meth.Ch	Large	1963
Degarwy	Wales	St.Mary	Candlesticks	1968
Deighton	Yorks.N	All Saints	Chair	1942
Dewsbury	Yorks.W	All Saints	Several	1951
Dewsbury	Yorks.W	Deaf and Dumb Inst.	Several	1935
Dewsbury	Yorks.W	Royal Photographic Soc	Few	1950
Dewsbury	Yorks.W	St.Marks	Several	1949
Dishforth	Yorks.N	Christchurch	Prayer Desk	1951
Dodworth	Yorks.S	St.John-t-Baptist	Few	1942
Dolphinholme	Lancs	St.Mark	Lectern	1967
Doncaster	Yorks.S	Cantley Methodist Ch	Plaque	1958
Doncaster	Yorks.S	St.George	Cred.Table	
Doncaster	Yorks.S	St.Mary	Few	1967
Doncaster	Yorks.S	Tech.High School for Girls	Lectern	1958
Dorchester	Dorset	Herrison Hospital	Few	1970
Dormanstown	Tees	All Saints	Few	1931
Dornoch	Scot.N	Cathedral	Cross	1996
Dortmund	Germ.	Roy.Art.Garrison	Table	1971
Dorton	Bucks	Ashfold School	Furniture	
Downside	Somset	Abbey	Several	1947
Drax	Yorks.E	Grammar School	Several	1940
Drax	Yorks.E	St.Peter & Paul	Several	1937
Driffield Great	Yorks.E	All Saints	Few	1950
Driffield Little	Yorks.E	St.Peter	Prayer Desk	1946
Drighlington	Yorks.W	St.Paul	Few	1956
Dringhouses	York	Presbyterian Ch	Several	1963
Dringhouses	York	St.Edwards	Several	1941
Drybergh,Kelso	Scot.S	Dryberg Abbey Hotel	Several	
Drypool	Yorks.E	St.John	Few	1934
Dunnington	Yorks.E	St.Nicholas	Several	1929
Durham	Durham	Ch	Missal stand	1964
Durham	Durham	Ch	Pews	1969
Durham	Durham	Cathedral	Few	1953
Durham	Durham	County Cricket Club	Board	
Durham	Durham	Durham Castle	Lectern	
Durham	Durham	Durham School	Several	1954
Durham	Durham	Hatfield College	Lecterns	1948
Durham	Durham	Lyons Chapel	Mem.Tablet	1952
Durham	Durham	Middlebrook	CredTable	1997
Durham	Durham	NFU Boardroom	Few	1956
Durham	Durham	St.Chad	Few	1934
Durham	Durham	St.Cuthbert	Cred Table	1996
Durham	Durham	St.Giles	Several	1936
Durham	Durham	St.Hilda	Few	1967
Durham	Durham	St.Hildas CE School	Oak Cross	1967
Durham	Durham	St.Margaret	Few	1997
Durham	Durham	St.Mary College	Large	1950
Durham	Durham	St.Oswald	Few	1965
Durham	Durham	Three Tuns	Furniture	1938
Durham	Durham	Ushaw College	Several	1937
Eaglescliffe	Tees	All Saints Preston	Large	1951
Eaglescliffe	Tees	Cleveland School	Few	1961
Earlsdon	Warks	St.Barbaras	Bench	1951
Earsdon	Tyne	St.Alban	Few	1958
Easby	Yorks.N	Ch	Tablet	1948
Easington	Durham	All Saints	Few	1942
Easington Colliery	Durham	Church of the Ascension	Several	1951
Easingwold	Yorks.N	All Saints & J-t-B	Several	1937
Easingwold	Yorks.N	Civil Defence School	Plaques	1953
Easingwold	Yorks.N	CofE School	Shield	1948
Easingwold	Yorks.N	Grammar School	Few	1947
Easingwold	Yorks.N	John Macauley	Shield	1996
Easingwold	Yorks.N	St.Mary	Several	1937
Easingwold	Yorks.N	The Cafe	Doors	1964
East Ardsley	Yorks.W	St.Gabriel	Few	1969
East Cawton	Yorks.N	Ch	Font Cover	

Place	Area	Site	Description	Earliest Date
East Cowton	Yorks.N	All Saints	Pew	2000
East Grinstead	Sussex	Alton Ho.	MemTablet	1961
East Grinstead	Sussex	St.Mary	Several	1942
East Grinstead	Surrey	St.Swithern	Doors	1926
East Harlsey	Yorks.N	St.Oswald	Several	1927
East Hestleton	Yorks.N	St.Andrew	Several	1997
East Keswick	Yorks.W	St.Mary	Large	1955
East Layton	Durham	Ch	Few	1961
East Malling	Kent	St.James	Several	1983
East Preston	Sussex	Our Lady Star of Sea	Lectern	1966
East Witton	Yorks.N	St.John-t-Evangelist	Few	1938
Eastend	Canada	St.Augustine	Table	
Easterside	Tees	St.Agnes	Cupboard	1981
Eastrington	Yorks.E	St.Michael	Candlesticks	1953
Ebberston	Yorks.N	St.Mary	Hymn Boards	1956
Edgbaston	Warks	Ch	Cross	1987
Edinburgh	Scot.C	Ch	CredTable	1989
Edinburgh	Scot.C	Ch	Font,	1952
Edmonton,Alberta	Canada	St.Peter Anglican Ch	Hymn Board	2004
Eggleston	Durham	Ch	Lectern	1952
Egton	Yorks.N	St.Hilda	Few	1969
Elgin	Scot.N	Gordonstoun School	Lectern	1954
Elland	Yorks.E	All Saints & St.Mary	Large	1968
Elland	Yorks.W	St.Mary	Several	1936
Ellesmere	Shrop	Ellesmere College	Several	1968
Elmbridge	Worcs	Ch	Cross	1938
Elmore,Speen	Berks	Elmore Abbey	Seating	1995
Elvington	Yorks.E	Holy Trinity	Several	1948
Ely	Cambs	St.David	CredTable	1949
Emley	Yorks.W	St.Michael	Few	1968
Escrick	York	Escrick Primary School	Few	1953
Esher	Surrey	Ch	Cross	1976
Eston	Tees	St.Chad	Large	1942
Eston	Tees	St.Helen	Several	1949
Eston	Tees	Christchurch	Screen	
Eymouth	NLand	All Saints	Staves	1940
Faceby	Yorks.N	St.Mary Mag	Several	1955
Fairfield	Derby	St.Peter	Staves	1941
Fairwater Cardiff	Wales	St.Peter	Several	1961
Fareham	Hants	Ch	Lectern	1965
Farington	Lancs	St.Paul	Few	1958
Farlington	York	Ch	Few	1943
Farne Islands	NLand	St.Cuthbert	Few	1933
Farnhill	Yorks.N	Moreton Hall, High Farnhill	Large	1937
Farnley	Yorks.W	Parish Ch	Several	1935
Farringdon	Durham	Holy Rosary Pres.	Large	2000
Farsley	Yorks.W	Ch	Screens	1955
Felixkirk	Yorks.N	St.Felix	Several	1929
Feltham	Midsex	Sparrow Farm Jun.Sch.	MemBoard	1982
Fence Houses	Durham	Ch	Chair	1939
Fenham	Tyne	St.James & Basil	Stand	1970
Ferryhill	Durham	St.Luke	Benches	1971
Ferryside	Wales	St.Thomas	Stalls	1959
Fir Tree	Durham	Duke of York Inn	Several	1967
Flamborough	Yorks.E	St.Oswald	Few	1966
Flaxton	Yorks.N	St.Lawrence	Several	1950
Fleet	Lincs	Cheshire Home	Few	1955
Fleetwood	Lancs	Rossall School	Several	1962
Follifoot	Yorks.W	Ch	Pulpit	1956
Forcett	Yorks.N	St.Cuthbert	Few	1950
Ford	NLand	The Manse	Seat	1953
Fort Augustus	Scot.N	St.Benedict's Abbey	Screen	1921
Fowey	Cornwall	Hospital	Bench	1980
Freckleton	Lancs	Clifton Arms Hotel	Bar	
Freckleton	Lancs	Holy Trinity	Few	1981
Fryston	Yorks.E	St.Peter's	Kneelers	1934
Fulneck	Yorks.W	Moravian Ch	Tablet	1999
Fulwood	Lancs	Carmelite Monastry	Chair	1966
Fylde	Ches	Fylde Lodge School	Platform Set	1961

Place	Area	Site	Description	Earliest Date
Gainford	Tees	Ch	Font	1984
Gambia	Gambia	Bishop of Gambia	Kneeler	1950
Gargrave	Yorks.N	St.Andrew	Several	1952
Garstang	Lancs	Chequered Flag Resturant	Furniture	
Gawber	Yorks.S	St.Thomas	Several	1983
Germany	Germ.	Alanbrooke Barracks Mess	Tables	1997
Giggleswick	Yorks.N	Woodlands Guest Ho.	Several	
Gilling	Yorks.N	Gilling Castle School	Large	1925
Gilling East	Yorks.N	Holy Cross	Few	1945
Gilling West	Yorks.N	Churchyard	Few	1938
Glanville Wootton	Dorset	Ch	Several	1956
Glastonbury	Somset	St.Andrew Edgavly	Several	1954
Goathland	Yorks.N	B V Mary	Several	1934
Gomersal	Yorks.W	Grove United Reform Ch	Few	1957
Gomersal	Yorks.W	St.Mary	Several	1948
Gosforth	Tyne	Newlands School	Few	1984
Gosforth	Tyne	Westfield School	Lectern	1999
Gosport	Hants	Ch	Cross	1983
Grahamstown	S.Africa	Cathedral	Tablets	1954
Grange-o-Sands	Lancs	Ch	Stall	1964
Grangetown	Tees	Ch	Several	1955
Grassendale	Lancs	St.Austin	Few	1938
Great Ayton	Yorks.N	Christchurch	Several	1950
Great Harrowden	Nhants	All Saints	Screen	1940
Great Houghton	Yorks.S	St.Michael&All Angels	Seating	1964
Great Malvern	Worcs	Priory	Seating	1958
Great Ouseburn	Yorks.N	St.Mary	Few	1914
Great Smeaton	Yorks.N	Ch	Few	1938
Green Hammerton	Yorks.N	Bay Horse Inn	Few	1966
Green Hammerton	Yorks.N	Cemetary	Gates	
Greenhow	Yorks.N	St.Mary	Few	1949
Gressingham	Lancs	Ch	Missal stand	2002
Grewelthorpe	Yorks.N	Ch	Reredos	
Grinkle Park	Yorks.N	Grinkle Park Hotel	Few	1930
Grinton	Yorks.N	St.Andrew	Tablet	1944
Grosmont	Yorks.N	St.Matthew	Altar	1947
Guisborough	Yorks.N	Ch	Few	1967
Guisborough	Yorks.N	Grammar School	Table	1961
Guisborough	Yorks.N	St.Columb	Few	1955
Gunnerside	Yorks.N	Gunnerside Lodge	Oak Room	1930
Hadley,Barnett	Herts	Hadley Common Rectory	RemCase	2003
Haigh	Lancs	Ch.	Statue	1922
Haileybury	Herts	Haileybury College	Furniture	1933
Halifax	Yorks.W	All Saints	Several	1948
Halifax	Canada	Cathedral	Pulpit	
Halifax	Yorks.W	Heath United Reform Ch.	ComTable	1997
Halifax	Yorks.W	Parish Ch	Panelling	1961
Halifax	Yorks.W	St.Augustine	Large	1949
Halifax	Yorks.W	St.Mark	Altar rails	1963
Halifax	Yorks.W	Wellesley Barracks	Chairs	1956
Hampsthwaite	Yorks.N	St.Thomas a Beckett	Several	1938
Hampton-in-Arden	Warks	St.Mary & Bartholomew	Cross	1969
Hamsterley	Durham	Vicarage	Few	1986
Hardraw	Yorks.N	St.Mary & John	Posts	1969
Harehills	Yorks.W	St.Stephen	Altar rails	1958
Harewood	Yorks.W	Ch	Few	1967
Harome	Yorks.N	Hotel	Fireplace	1946
Harome	Yorks.N	St.Saviour	Altar rails	1911
Harome	Yorks.N	Star Inn	Large	1934
Harrogate	Yorks.N	Ch	Sanc.Chairs	1950
Harrogate	Yorks.N	Ch	Pews	1956
Harrogate	Yorks.N	Ch	Lectern	1964
Harrogate	Yorks.N	Ch	Board	1996
Harrogate	Yorks.N	Austin Reed's Shop	Several	
Harrogate	Yorks.N	Avenue Hotel	Several	1938
Harrogate	Yorks.N	Baptist Ch	Several	1962
Harrogate	Yorks.N	Bettys Cafe	Several	1998
Harrogate	Yorks.N	Birklands School	Lectern	1966
Harrogate	Yorks.N	Christchurch	Altar Rails	1936
Harrogate	Yorks.N	Dukes Bar	Bar	1968
Harrogate	Yorks.N	Education Office	Crick.Shield	1950
Harrogate	Yorks.N	Girls High School	Boards	1966
Harrogate	Yorks.N	Harlow Hill Methodist	Large	1939
Harrogate	Yorks.N		Several	1938
Harrogate	Yorks.N	Harrogate College	Several	1938
Harrogate	Yorks.N	Hosp.Dist. & Gen.Chapel	Large	1930
Harrogate	Yorks.N	Ladies College	Several	1955
Harrogate	Yorks.N	Oakdale School	Library	1939
Harrogate	Yorks.N	Old Swan Inn	Few	1966
Harrogate	Yorks.N	Queen Ethelburgas Sch.	Several	1962
Harrogate	Yorks.N	Robinson Hall Children Home	Few	1961
Harrogate	Yorks.N	Scout Council	Lectern	1971
Harrogate	Yorks.N	Squinting Cat	Stools	1965
Harrogate	Yorks.N	St Aelred	Altar rails	1968
Harrogate	Yorks.N	St.George House	Mem.Board	
Harrogate	Yorks.N	St.Leonard	ComTable	1994
Harrogate	Yorks.N	St.Luke	Several	1960
Harrogate	Yorks.N	St.Mark	Prayer desk	1949
Harrogate	Yorks.N	St.Martins Prep Sch.	Bookcases	1969
Harrogate	Yorks.N	St.Mary	Several	1946
Harrogate	Yorks.N	St.Peter	Several	1944
Harrogate	Yorks.N	St.Robert	Few	1936
Harrogate	Yorks.N	St.Wilfrid	Several	1936
Harrogate	Yorks.N	Stonefall Cem.Chapel	Large	1936
Harrogate	Yorks.N	Technical School	Lectern	1962
Harrogate	Yorks.N	Trinity Methodist	Few	1958
Harrogate	Yorks.N	Victoria Park Methodist	Few	1947
Harrogate	Yorks.N	Yorks.Agric.Soc.	Chair	
Hartburn	Tees	West End Bowling Club	Trophy	
Hartlepool	Durham	Business LinkTeesvalley	Chair	1998
Hartlepool	Durham	Ch	Table	1953
Hartlepool	Durham	Ch	Kneelers	1967
Hartlepool	Durham	Ch	Pews	1969
Hartlepool	Durham	Greatham Hospital	Seating	1962
Hartlepool	Durham	Holy Trinity	Few	1961
Hartlepool	Durham	Presb.Ch	Several	1953
Hartlepool	Durham	St.Luke	Several	1948
Hartlepool	Durham	St.Paul	Few	1960
Hartlepool	Durham	St.Peter	Several	1948
Hartlepool	Durham	Vicarage	Missal stand	1965
Hartshead	Yorks.W	St.Peter	Few	1968
Hassocks	Sussex	Ch	Lectern	1953
Hatfield	Herts	Queenswood Girls School	Benches	1987
Haughton-le-Skerne	Tees	NFU	Boards	1955
Haughton-le-Skerne	Tees	St.Andrew	Few	1952
Haverfordwest	Wales	Ch(Prendergast)	Several	1955
Haverfordwest	Wales	St.Martin	Large	1962
Haverfordwest	Wales	St.Mary	Several	1953
Hawes	Yorks.N	St.Margaret	Several	1955
Hawkesworthwood	Yorks.W	St.Mary	Several	1953
Hawnby	Yorks.N	All Saints	CredTable	1995
Haworth	Yorks.W	Junior School	MemBoard	1982
Haworth	Yorks.W	Our Lady of Lourdes	Few	2001
Hawthorn	Durham	St.Michael & All Angels	Altar	1965
Haxby	York	St.Thomas	Few	1949
Headingley	Yorks.W	Bishop House	Altar	1989
Headingley	Yorks.W	Golf Club	Few	1986
Headingley	Yorks.W	Methodist	Several	1937
Headingley	Yorks.W	St.Chad	Several	1951
Headingley	Yorks.W	St.Michael	Several	1937
Healey, Masham	Yorks.N	St.Paul	Table	1968
Hebden Bridge	Yorks.W	St.James	Several	1949
Hebden Bridge	Yorks.W	St.John	Several	1935
Heckmondwike	Yorks.W	St.Saviour	Lectern	1967
Helensburgh	Scot.C	St.Michael	Seating	
Helmsley	Yorks.N	All Saints	Several	1930
Helmsley	Yorks.N	Catholic Ch	Tabernacle	1958
Helmsley	Yorks.N	Cemetary	Few	1929
Helmsley	Yorks.N	Duncombe Park	Several	1956

Altar and reredos with linenfold panelling installed at Goathland parish church in 1934.

Choir or pew front, with pierced tracery and carved rosettes, completed for Howden Minster in 1932.

Place	Area	Site	Description	Earliest Date
Helmsley	Yorks.N	Feathers Hotel	Bar	1963
Helmsley	Yorks.N	Masonic Lodge	Chair	1965
Helmsley	Yorks.N	Methodists	Table	
Helmsley	Yorks.N	N.Yorks Moors Nat.Park	Plaque	1989
Helmsley	Yorks.N	Q.Marys Sch.Duncombe Pk	Several	1938
Helperby	Yorks.N	Ch	Memorial	1963
Hemel Hempstead	Herts	Ch	Pew	1998
Hemingbrough	Yorks.E	St.Mary	Several	1947
Hertford	Herts	Hertingfordawry St.Mary	Cross	2001
Hertford	Herts	St.John	Missal stand	1965
Hessle	Yorks.E	Methodist Ch	Few	2003
Hetton-le-Hole	Durham	St.Nicholas	Stools	1969
Heworth	York	St.James	Few	1962
Heworth	York	St.Wulstan	Large	1940
Hexham	NLand	Albert Edward Club	Furniture	1984
Highgate	London	St.Michael	Chair	1953
High Melton	Yorks.S	St.James	Few	1969
Hillington	Norfolk	Church Uphall	Altar	1937
Hitchin	Herts	Girls' Grammar School	Few	1960
Hitchin	Herts	St.Mary	Several	1952
Hoddlesden	Lancs	St.Paul	Few	1948
Holbeck	Yorks.W	St.Matthew	Several	1932
Hollinwood	Lancs	Ch	Several	1947
Holloway	Derby	Christ Ch	Stand	
Holme Valley	Yorks.W	Ch	Few	1965
Holme-o-SM	Yorks.E	All Saints Spalding Moor	Several	1938
Holtby	Yorks.N	Holy Trinity	Several	1936
Holy Island	NLand	Ch	Few	1940
Honiara	Solomon Is.	Parliament Buildings	Chair	1995
Honley	Yorks.W	St.Mary	Tablets	1948
Hook	Lincs	St.Mary	Board	1998
Hope	Derby	St.Peter	Stalls	
Hopton Mirfield	Yorks.W	Congregational Ch	Few	1950
Horbury	Yorks.W	St.Mary & St.John Convent	Large	1963
Horbury	Yorks.W	St.Peter Convent	Large	1965
Horbury Junction	Yorks.W	Msrs Chas.Roberts Ltd	Several	1956
Horbury Junction	Yorks.W	St.Mary	Altar rails	1965
Hornby	Yorks.N	Ch	CredTable	1994
Hornsea	Yorks.E	Ch	Several	1936
Hornsea	Yorks.E	Sacred Heart	Candlesticks	1997
Horsforth	Yorks.W	Ch	Few	1920
Horsforth	Yorks.W	Frobelian School	Library	1963
Horsehouse	Yorks.N	Ch	CredTable	1946
Horsham	Sussex	Ch	Carving	1980
Hovingham	Yorks.N	St.Stephen	Few	1937
Hovingham	Yorks.N	Hovingham Hall	Tablets	1937
Howden	Yorks.E	Bishops Palace	Few	1938
Howden	Yorks.E	Minster St.Peter	Large	1932
Howsham	Yorks.N	Ch	Gates	1948
Hoyland	Yorks.S	Sacred Heart & St.Helen	Chair	1929
Hubberholme	Yorks.N	St Mic. & All Angels	Several	1933
Huddersfield	Yorks.W	Ch	Few	1958
Huddersfield	Yorks.W	Crosland Moor	Few	1987
Huddersfield	Yorks.W	Dalton	Dishes	1999
Huddersfield	Yorks.W	Fine Worsteds Ltd	Tablet	1954
Huddersfield	Yorks.W	Fixby	Tablet	1950
Huddersfield	Yorks.W	Hillhouse Cong. Ch	Few	1969
Huddersfield	Yorks.W	Holmfirth	Few	2000
Huddersfield	Yorks.W	Holmfirth Masonic Lodge	Chair	
Huddersfield	Yorks.W	Holy Trinity	Several	1944
Huddersfield	Yorks.W	Learoyd Bros. Ironwks	Several	1951
Huddersfield	Yorks.W	St.Bridgits	Several	1993
Huddersfield	Yorks.W	St.James Unit.Ref.Ch	Table	1983
Huddersfield	Yorks.W	St.Mary	Lectern	1948
Huddersfield	Yorks.W	St.Michael	Few	1970
Huddersfield	Yorks.W	St.Peter	Several	1944
Huddersfield	Yorks.W	St.Stephen Lindley	Lectern	1950
Huddersfield	Yorks.W	Technical College	Mem.Chair	1953
Huddersfield	Yorks.W	Trafalgar Mills	Tablet	1954
Huddersfield	Yorks.W	United Reform Moldgreen	Few	
Hull	Yorks.E	Andrew Marvell High Sch.	Lectern	1969
Hull	Yorks.E	Bishop of Hull	Staff	1945
Hull	Yorks.E	Holy Trinity	Several	1935
Hull	Yorks.E	Presbyterian Ch,Baker St	Table	1960
Hull	Yorks.E	Scout Assoc.	Cross	1983
Hull	Yorks.E	Spillers Ltd	Bookcase	1959
Hull	Yorks.E	St.Augustine	Several	1950
Hull	Yorks.E	St.Cuthbert	Several	1956
Hull	Yorks.E	St.John	Several	1932
Hull	Yorks.E	St.Mary Eldon Grove	Few	1951
Hull	Yorks.E	University	Chair	1955
Hull	Yorks.E	Wayne Ch	Screens	1974
Huncoat	Lancs	St.Augustine	Several	1953
Hunmanby	Yorks.E	Hunmanby Hall School	Several	1930
Hunstanton	Norfolk	Glebe House School	Several	1961
Huntington	York	St.Andrew	Several	1939
Hurley	Berks	St.Mary	Altar	1980
Hurworth	Tees	St.Cuthberts Hosp.	Several	1970
Husbands Bosworth	Warks	All Saints	Few	1962
Husthwaite	Yorks.N	St.Nicholas	Several	1920
Hutton Buscel	Yorks.N	St.Matthew	Several	1935
Hutton Magna	Durham	Ch	Lych Gate	1920
Hutton Rudby	Yorks.N	All Saints	Few	1958
Hutton Rudby	Yorks.N	Methodist Ch	Few	1997
Hutton-le-Hole	Yorks.N	St.Chad	Few	1934
Huyton	Lancs	Ch	Few	1966
Hyde	Ches	Holy Trinity Gee Cross	Several	1961
Hythe	Kent	Sch.of Inf.,Marlsford Ch	Few	1948
Ickham	Kent	Ch	Tablet	1935
Idle	Yorks.W	Congregational Ch	Several	1946
Idle	Yorks.W	St.Cuthbert	Lectern	
Ilford	Essex	Valentines High School	Board	1983
Ilkeston	Leics	St.Mary	Hymn Boards	1969
Ilkley	Yorks.W	Ch	Lectern	1963
Ilkley	Yorks.W	Ch	Plates	1967
Ilkley	Yorks.W	Ch	Board	2001
Ilkley	Yorks.W	All Saints	Few	1953
Ilkley	Yorks.W	Christian Scientists	Tablets	1951
Ilkley	Yorks.W	Col.of Housecraft	Several	1956
Ilkley	Yorks.W	Grammar School	Lectern	1962
Ilkley	Yorks.W	St.Margaret	Large	1934
Ilkley	Yorks.W	St.Mary	Few	1964
Ilmington	Warks	St.Mary	Large	1938
Indianapolis	USA	Trinity Ch	Alms Box	1959
Ingleby Arncliffe	Yorks.N	All Saints	Altar rails	1926
Ingleby Arncliffe	Yorks.N	School	Plaque	1953
Ingleby Greenhow	Yorks.N	St.Andrew	Few	1949
Ingleton	Yorks.W	St.Mary	Several	1954
Ingsdon	Devon	Convent Holy Ghost	Tablet	1958
Ipswich	Suffolk	Ch	Statue	1955
Ipswich	Essex	St.Edmonds Road	Kneeler	1953
Isle of Ensay,Harris	Scot.N	Private Chapel	Door	
Jarrow	Tyne	Bishop of Jarrow	Several	1965
Jedburgh	Scot.S	Oxnam Kirk	Several	1997
Jervaulx	Yorks.N	Ch	Chest	1938
Jesmond	Tyne	St.John	Missal stand	1954
Katmandu	Nepal	Parliament	Chairs	1992
Keighley	Yorks.W	Ch	Lectern	1982
Keighley	Yorks.W	Long Lee Methodists	Chairs	1972
Keighley	Yorks.W	St.Andrew	Stands	1968
Keighley	Yorks.W	St.Mark	Chair	1980
Kelloe	Durham	St.Helen	Chairs	1998
Kepwick	Yorks.N	Ch	Few	1938
Keswick	Cumbria	Ch	Few	1928
Kettering	NHants	St.Andrew	Few	2004
Kettlewell	Yorks.N	Manor House	Several	1938
Kettlewell	Yorks.N	St.Mary	Panelling	1937
Kidderminster	Worcs	Town Hall	Furniture	1958

Place	Area	Site	Description	Earliest Date
Kilburn	Yorks.N	Forresters Arms	Several	1965
Kilburn	Yorks.N	St.Mary	Large	1925
Kilburn	Yorks.N	Village Square	Benches	1921
Kildale	Yorks.N	Ch	Altar rails	1962
Kildwick	Yorks.W	St.Andrew	Candlesticks	1962
Killinghall	Yorks.N	Ch	Screen	1938
Killinghall	Yorks.N	Dr.Barnardos Home	Mem.Panel	1952
Killinghall	Yorks.N	St.Johns Ambulance Hall	Few	1967
Kilvington S.	Yorks.N	St.Wilfrid	Few	1926
Kingsbridge	Devon	St.Edmunds	Mem.Table	1967
Kingswinsford	Worcs	Holy Trinity	Gates	
Kinsley	Yorks.W	Ascension Ch	Chairs	1961
Kippax	Yorks.N	St.Mary	Altar rails	1955
Kirby Knowle	Yorks.N	St.Wilfrid	Several	1935
Kirby Misperton	Yorks.N	St.Lawrence	Few	1931
Kirby Wiske	Yorks.N	Ch	Several	1919
Kirk Bramwith	Yorks.S	St.Mary	Large	1935
Kirk Deighton	Yorks.W	All Saints	Few	1949
Kirk Deighton	Yorks.W	Village Green	Sign	1955
Kirk Ella	Yorks.E	Cemetary Ch	Few	1941
Kirk Hammerton	Yorks.N	St.John	Several	1946
Kirk Levington	Yorks.N	St.Martin	Few	1938
Kirkburton	Yorks.W	All Hallows	Case	1957
Kirkby Fleetham	Yorks.N	St.Andrews	Chairs	1995
Kirkby Fleetham	Yorks.N	The Hall	Kneelers	1949
Kirkby Lonsdale	Cumbria	Casterton School	Few	1952
Kirkby Lonsdale	Cumbria	Ch	Pascal sticks	1998
Kirkby Malham	Yorks.N	St.Michael & James	Table	1937
Kirkby Malzeard	Yorks.N	St.Andrew	Large	1937
Kirkby Overblow	Yorks.N	All Saints	Several	1940
Kirkby Ravensworth	Cumbria	St.Peter & Felix	Several	1958
Kirkby-in-Cleveland	Yorks.N	St.Augustine	Several	1948
Kirkbymoorside	Yorks.N	Hexthorpe	Font	1964
Kirkbymoorside	Yorks.N	Hospital	Several	1949
Kirkbymoorside	Yorks.N	Ryedale Printing Works	Boardroom	2007
Kirkbymoorside	Yorks.N	St.Chad	Several	1961
Kirkbymoorside	Yorks.N	Welburn Hall School	Several	1963
Kirkdale	Yorks.N	St.Gregory's Minster	Chair	1937
Kirkham	Lancs	Grammar School	Several	1958
Kirkheaton	Yorks.W	St.John the Baptist	Stall	1964
Kirkleavington,Yarm	Tees	St.Martin	Few	1936
Kirkthorpe	Yorks.W	St.Peter	Few	1957
Knaresborough	Yorks.N	Castle	Court Rm	1957
Knaresborough	Yorks.N	Ch	Staff	1957
Knaresborough	Yorks.N	Ch	Font	1968
Knaresborough	Yorks.N	Ch	Table	1995
Knaresborough	Yorks.N	Ch	Few	2000
Knaresborough	Yorks.N	Holy Trinity	Several	1952
Knaresborough	Yorks.N	Nidd Vale Masonic Lodge	Chair	
Knaresborough	Yorks.N	St.John-t-Baptist	Several	1944
Knighton	Wales	Vicarage	Prayer Desk	1964
Lanchester	Durham	All Saints	Several	1939
Langthorpe	Yorks.N	Ch	Mem.Board	
Langton	Yorks.N	St.Andrew	Few	1935
Larkhill	Wilts	Royal Sch. of Artillery Ch	Prayer Desk	1998
Lastingham	Yorks.N	St.Mary	Few	1956
Leake	Yorks.N	Ch (from Bridlington)	Few	1933
Leamington Spa	Warks	Warwickshire College	Library	1996
Leathley	Yorks.W	St.Oswald	Large	1948
Leconfield	Yorks.E	St.Catherine	Few	1979
Leeds	Yorks.W	Ch	Staves	1952
Leeds	Yorks.W	Ch	Lectern	1964
Leeds	Yorks.W	Ch	Panelling	1961
Leeds	Yorks.W	Ch	Missal stand	1961
Leeds	Yorks.W	Ch	Lectern	1965
Leeds	Yorks.W	Ch	Chairs	1969
Leeds	Yorks.W	All Hallows St.Simon	Few	1962
Leeds	Yorks.W	All Saints	Few	1938
Leeds	Yorks.W	Alwoodley Golf Club	Mem.Tab.	1940
Leeds	Yorks.W	Bishop's House	Several	1939
Leeds	Yorks.W	Briamwood High School	Plaque	1997
Leeds	Yorks.W	Ch.of Ascension	Cross	1969
Leeds	Yorks.W	Christchurch	Canopy	1951
Leeds	Yorks.W	Cockburn High School	Lectern	1950
Leeds	Yorks.W	Convent of Holy Child	Plaque	1961
Leeds	Yorks.W	Elmete Hall School	Lectern	1963
Leeds	Yorks.W	Girls High School	Library	1933
Leeds	Yorks.W	Grammar School	Chair	1935
Leeds	Yorks.W	J.Wilby&Sons Ltd	Tablet	1965
Leeds	Yorks.W	Oxford Place Chapel	Table	1960
Leeds	Yorks.W	Premier Motor Auction	Tables	1999
Leeds	Yorks.W	Publicity Ch	Lectern	1961
Leeds	Yorks.W	School of Medicine	Several	1936
Leeds	Yorks.W	St.Aidan	Screen	1949
Leeds	Yorks.W	St.Chad	Plates	1962
Leeds	Yorks.W	St.Cross	Several	1971
Leeds	Yorks.W	St.James Hospital Chapel	Several	1961
Leeds	Yorks.W	St.John the Evangelist	Board	2001
Leeds	Yorks.W	St.Margaret	Several	1945
Leeds	Yorks.W	St.Martin	Font cover	1961
Leeds	Yorks.W	St.Mary	Lectern	1950
Leeds	Yorks.W	St.Matthew	Kneeler	1955
Leeds	Yorks.W	St.Matthias	Few	1961
Leeds	Yorks.W	St.Poskitt	Kneelers	1939
Leeds	Yorks.W	St.Stephen	Altar rails	1957
Leeds	Yorks.W	St.Wilfrid	Altar rails	
Leeds	Yorks.W	TOC H,Brotherton House	Cross	1936
Leeds	Yorks.W	Wesley College	Few	1934
Leeds	Yorks.W	West High School	Mem.Board	
Leeds	Yorks.W	Yorks. Archeological Soc.	Cradle	1939
Leeds	Yorks.W	Yorks. Copper Works	Furniture	1939
Leeds	Yorks.W	Yorkshire Post Publicity Club	Missal stand	1962
Leeds	Yorks.W	Convent L S of Poor	Various	
Leek	Staffs	Westwood Hall GH School	Lectern	1960
Leeming	Yorks.N	RAF Station Offi. Mess	Large	1940
Leeming	Yorks.N	St.Michael	Altar rails	1941
Leeming Bar	Yorks.N	Dale Pack Food Ltd.	Boardroom	
Leicester	Leics	Ch	Cross	1996
Leicester	Leics	Grand Hotel Simon's Bar	Pews	
Leicester	Leics	Gt.Glen Vicarage	Benches	1957
Leicester	Leics	St.Mary's Ironworks	Desk	1939
Leigh	Lancs	Ch	Rem.Case	1957
Leigh-o-Sea	Essex	St.Michaels School	Few	1999
Leominster	Hereford	Powell	Eagle Lectern	1981
Levisham	Yorks.N	St.John the Baptist	Several	1946
Leyburn	Yorks.N	St.Matthew	Several	1940
Leyburn	Yorks.N	St.Peter and Paul	Altar rails	1936
Leyland	Lancs	St.Marys Priory	Large	1964
Leyton	Lancs	Ch	Altar rails	1955
Leyton	Essex	Ch	Several	1958
Limpsfield	Notts	St.Andrew	Benches	1970
Linton	Yorks.W	Memorial Hall	Plaque	1996
Linton	Yorks.W	St.Michael	Several	1951
Linton	Yorks.W	Woodhall Centre	Large	
Linton-on-Ouse	Yorks.N	RAFOfficers Mess	Bar	1940
Lisburn	NI	8th Inf.Brig.Garrison Ch	MemTable	1989
Littleborough	Lancs	Ch	Board	1970
Liverpool	Lancs	Ch	Table	1962
Liverpool	Lancs	Ch	Chest	1963
Liverpool	Lancs	Mossley Hill	Box	1963
Liverpool	Lancs	St.Austin	Figures	1956
Liverpool	Lancs	St.Dominics Sec.Sch.	Statue	1964
Liverpool	Lancs	St.Francis Xavier	Kneelers	1954
Liverpool	Lancs	St.Mary-t-V,Waterloo Pk	Few	1936
Liverpool	Lancs	St.Philomenas J School	Statue	1957
Liverpool	Lancs	The Manse	Cupboard	1981
Liverpool	Lancs	Welch Presbyterian Ch	Lectern	1957
Liverton	Yorks.N	St.Martin	Candlesticks	1966

Place	Area	Site	Description	Earliest Date
Llandaff	Wales	Cathedral	Altar rails	1960
Llanddaniel	Wales	Ch	Few	1963
Llandinam	Wales	Broneirion GG Centre	Several	1953
Llandudno	Wales	Holy Trinity	Few	1962
Llanllowell	Wales	St.Llywell	Various	
Loftus	Yorks.N	St.Leonard	Several	1933
Loftus	Yorks.N	UDC Offices	Board	1973
Londesborough	Yorks.N	All Saints	Cross	1946
London	London	All Saints Fulham	Stalls	
London	London	Assumption,Warwick St.	Table	
London	London	Austin Reed's Shop	Several	
London	London	Ben Johnson Printers	Boardroom	
London	London	Brentwood	Seating	1967
London	London	Church Ho. Westminster	Tables	1933
London	London	DFox&CoLtd	Boardroom	1971
London	London	Ealing Abbey	Few	1964
London	London	Ellis & Co Ltd	Few	1971
London	London	Esher College	Few	
London	London	Hammerslane	Few	1988
London	London	Henrietta Barnett School	Few	1964
London	London	Imp.Canc.Research Centre	Bookcase	
London	London	Inc.Accountants Hall	Mem.Font	1953
London	London	Insurance Hall	Lectern	1999
London	London	Investment Intelligence Ltd	Several	1970
London	London	London House,Bloomsbury	Large	1937
London	London	MCC at Lords	Lords Plaque	1955
London	London	Midland BankThreadn.St.	Table	1964
London	London	NFU Knightsbridge	Tables	1983
London	London	Our Lady/Rosary Marylebone	Few	1964
London	London	Hampstead Ch	Chairs	2005
London	London	Hillingdon Ch	Altar	1938
London	London	Richmond Ch	Several	1949
London	London	Police College Hendon	Candelabra	1939
London	London	Police Federation Surbiton	Bookcases	1983
London	London	Reeds School Watford	Few	1940
London	London	Residential College W1	Several	1967
London	London	Royal College of Nursing	Few	1963
London	London	Royal Oceanic Racing Club	Bar stools	1936
London	London	Royal Photo.Soc.	Few	1951
London	London	St.Benedicts School Ealing	Library	1956
London	London	St.Dunstans Cheam	Lectern	1958
London	London	St.Edward Addington	Large	1958
London	London	St.George Hospital	Chairs	1963
London	London	St.George Tooting Grove	Seating	
London	London	St.Mary Fulham	Few	1951
London	London	St.Mary Waterloo	Several	1935
London	London	St.Mary Wimbledon	Bench	1993
London	London	St.Mary Hampstead	Several	1942
London	London	St.Mary/Etou Hackney Wick	Stools	1944
London	London	St.Marys School Barnes	Board	1995
London	London	St.Michael Highgate	Few	1957
London	London	St.Paul, Mill Hill	Prayer Desks	
London	London	Trustee Savings Bank	Boardroom	1967
London	London	Twickenham	Few	1996
London	London	Wax Chandlers' Hall	Few	1972
London	London	Westminster Abbey	Several	1941
Long Marton	Cumbria	Ch	Board	1999
Long Sutton	Lincs	Court House, Phoenix Ho.	Few	1965
Longton	Lancs	St.Andrew	Several	1954
Longwood	Yorks.W	St.Mark	Few	1949
Lothersdale	Yorks.W	Christ Ch	Few	1938
Low Fell	Tyne	St.John	Prayer Desk	1964
Lowick	NLand	St.John	Candlesticks	1950
Luddenden	Yorks.W	Ch	Altar rails	1962
Lundwood	Yorks.S	St.Mary Mag	Few	1966
Lupset	Yorks.W	Ch	Few	1948
Lymington,Ayr	Scot.S	Ch	Prayer Desks	1957
Lynton	Devon	Lee Abbey Fellowship	Stands	1965
Lytham St.Annes	Lancs	Ansdell Co.Prim.Sch.	Table	1967
Lytham St.Annes	Lancs	St.Cuthbert	Few	1966
Macclesfield	Ches	Ch	Reredos	1939
Malton	Yorks.N	Ch	Lectern	1965
Malton	Yorks.N	Green Man Hotel	Bar	1935
Malton	Yorks.N	St.Leonard	Few	1920
Malton	Yorks.N	St.Michael	Several	1951
Malton	Yorks.N	Town Hall	Few	1965
Malton	Yorks.N	Wesleyan Chapel	Several	1947
Malton Old	Yorks.N	St.Mary's Priory	Large	1931
Malvern Link	Worcs	St.Matthias	Few	1935
Manchester	Lancs	Ch	Hymn Boards	2001
Manchester	Lancs	Middleton Rectory	Staff	1944
Manchester	Lancs	Northern Baptist College	Several	1964
Manchester	Lancs	Ship Canal Ho.ICI Chancel	Few	1957
Manchester	Lancs	St.Peter RC Newall Green	Pulpit	1962
Manchester	Lancs	Taylor,Brown and Miller Co.	Tables	1964
Manchester	Lancs	Wm.Hulme Gram.Sch.	Hymn Board	1955
Manitoba	Canada	Ch	Few	1963
Manningham	Yorks.W	St.Paul	Tablet	1952
Manorbier	Wales	Ch	Large	1958
Market Weighton	Yorks.E	All Saints	Several	1941
Marlborough	Wilts	East Grafton Ch	Prayer Desk	1997
Marlesford	Suffolk	St.Andrew	Lectern	
Martindale	Cumbria	St.Peter	Gate	1963
Martock	Somset	All Saints	Altar	1961
Marton	Tees	St.Cuthbert	Large	1935
Marton-le-Moor	Yorks.N	Ch	Several	1949
Maryport	Cumbria	Ch	MemTablet	1954
Masham	Yorks.N	St.Mary	Tables	1950
Masham	Yorks.N	Swinton Conservative Col.	MemBoard	1963
Matlock	Derby	Ch	Several	1960
Maunby,Thirsk	Yorks.N	Burgess Sons	Office	1999
Mayland	Essex	Ch.	Cred.Table	1929
Meanwood	Yorks.W	Holy Trinity	Several	1961
Menston	Yorks.W	St.John the Divine	Large	1948
Methil, Fife	Scot.C	Ch	Large	1925
Methley	Yorks.S	St.Oswald	Several	1928
Mexborough	Yorks.S	Grammar School	Missal stand	1955
Mexborough	Yorks.S	St.John the Baptist	Several	1957
Middleham	Yorks.N	St.Mary & Alkelda	Altar rails	1950
Middlesbrough	Tees	Amos Hinton and Sons	Chair	1968
Middlesbrough	Tees	High School for Boys	Few	1960
Middlesbrough	Tees	South Bank Ch	Several	1937
Middlesbrough	Tees	St Barnabus Linthorpe	Large	1961
Middlesbrough	Tees	St.Cuthbert	Several	1953
Middlesbrough	Tees	St.George Linthorpe	Few	1955
Middlesbrough	Tees	St.John	Several	1951
Middlesbrough	Tees	St.Joseph	Several	1938
Middlesbrough	Tees	St.Marys School Acklam	Several	1952
Middlesbrough	Tees	St.Michael	CredTable	1949
Middlesbrough	Tees	St.Oswald Grove Hill Meths	Several	1934
Middlesbrough	Tees	St.Philomens Prestbytery	Candlesticks	1953
Middlesbrough	Tees	St.Thomas Brambles Farm	Few	1944
Middlesbrough	Tees	West Acklam Vicarage	Few	1958
Middlesbrough	Tees	Wynyard Park Prim.Sch.	Plaque	1964
Middleton	Norfolk	Ch	Medium	1965
Middleton Tyas	Yorks.N	St.Michael & All Angels	Several	1956
Middleton-i-Teesdale	Durham	Ch	Table	1970
Midhurst	Sussex	St.Mary Mag. & Dennis	Lectern	1998
Milford	Surrey	Ch	Grave Cross	1953
Millington	Yorks.E	St.Margaret	Few	1943
Milngavie	Scot.C	School?	Lectern	1961
Milnsbridge	Yorks.W	St.Luke Baptist Chapel	Several	1931
Minskip	Yorks.N	Mission Room	Few	1950
Mirfield	Yorks.W	Battyeford Ch	Few	1947
Mirfield	Yorks.W	Zion Baptist Ch	Lectern	1955
Mitchell	Cornwall	Ch	Angels	1948
Mitford Morpeth	NLand	St.Matthew	Staves	1965
Moffat	Scot.S	St.John the Evangelist	Few	1950

Screen and monks or priests' stalls at Methil, Fife. The central seat with its more elaborate carving was probably intended for the bishop or abbot. The unusual table has round legs that echo the design of the spindles in the screen.

Paschal candlesticks, dating from 1931, at Milnsbridge parish church, near Huddersfield. The exceptionally detailed carving would be both difficult and time-consuming.

Place	Area	Site	Description	Earliest Date
Moniac Castle	Scot.N	Private RC Chapel	Few	1933
Monk Fryston	Yorks.W	Prebendal Ho.	Door	1969
Monken Hadley	Herts	St.Mary Virgin	Several	1966
Monkwearmouth	Durham	All Saints	Several	1941
Monroe,Michigan	USA	Lutheran Home	Several	1995
Moor Monkton	York	Red House School	Few	1954
Moortown,Leeds	Yorks.W	Baptist Ch	Several	1953
Morecambe	Lancs	Christ Ch Cong.	Few	1964
Morecambe	Lancs	St.Patrick	Seating	
Morley	Yorks.W	St.Bridgits Churwell	Few	1966
Morpeth	NLand	Ch	Candlesticks	1969
Mortimer	Berks	Fitzherbert	Prayer Desks	1962
Mottram-in-LDD	Lancs	St.Michael Longdendale	Altar rail	
Mountain Ash	Wales	St.Margaret	Several	1963
Muker	Yorks.N	St.Mary	Lectern	
Murton	Durham	Holy Trinity	Several	1968
Murton	Yorks.E	St.James	Front	1974
Mytholmroyd	Yorks.W	St.Michael	Statue	1963
Nafferton	Yorks.N	All Saints	Several	1950
Nairn	Scot.N	St.Andrew	Few	1936
Nantwich	Ches	Rectory	Chairs	1981
Narborough	Leics	All Saints	Several	1949
Nassau	Bahamas	Christchurch Cathedral	Font Cover	1965
Nateby	Lancs	New Hotel	Several	1930
Nawton	Yorks.N	St.Gregory Minster	Few	1946
Neston	Ches	Vicarage	Chair	1963
Netherthong	Yorks.W	All Saints	Several	1960
Netherton	Yorks.W	Ch	Few	1973
Nevilles Cross	Durham	St.John	Several	1935
New Addington	Surrey	St.Edward-t-K+C	Large	1958
New Barnett	Herts	Ch	Few	2000
New Brighton	Ches	All Saints	Seats	1928
New Earswick	York	Jos.Rowntree Folk Hall	Shelter	1954
New Farnley	Yorks.W	St.James	Chairs	1995
New Mills	Ches	Vicarage	Chest	1957
New Ollerton	Notts	St.Joseph	Several	1929
Newburgh	Yorks.N	Newburgh Priory	Few	1944
Newby	Yorks.N	St.Mark	Lectern	
Newcastle	Tyne	7th Day Adventist	Table	1968
Newcastle	Tyne	Cathedral St.Nicholas	Large	1939
Newcastle	Tyne	Dame Allens School	Lectern	1951
Newcastle	Tyne	Holy Trinity	Missal stand	1966
Newcastle	Tyne	Northumberland Golf Club	Chairs	1988
Newcastle	Tyne	Royal Victoria Blind Sch.	Lectern	1961
Newcastle	Tyne	Rutherford Grammar School	Platform Set	1948
Newcastle	Tyne	St.Andrew	Several	1959
Newcastle	Tyne	St.Dominic Priory	Benches	1958
Newcastle	Tyne	St.John	Large	1935
Newcastle	Tyne	St.Patrick Rowlands Gill	Several	1984
Newcastle	Tyne	Univ.Dental Inst.	Few	1976
Newport	Wales	Cathedral St.Woollos	Large	1963
Newton	NLand	National Childrens Home	Lectern	1954
Newton	Lincs	Rectory	Alms Box	1955
Newton Aycliffe	Durham	St.Clare	Several	1966
Newton Green	Suffolk	All Saints	Candlesticks	
Newton,Pickering	Yorks.N	Ch	Settle	2001
Newton-o-Rawcliffe	Yorks.N	St.John	Altar rails	1939
Newton-u-Roseberry	Yorks.N	Ch	Few	1967
Nigg	Scot.N	Ch	Several	1935
Normanton	Yorks.W	All Saints	Stalls	1938
Normanton	Yorks.W	St.Mary	Font Cover	1939
North Cave	Yorks.E	Wesleyan Ch	Few	1939
North Ferriby	Yorks.E	All Saints	Several	1950
North Grimston	Yorks.N	Ch	Candlesticks	1946
North Kilworth	Leics	Ch	Altar	1995
North Ormsby	Tees	Holy Trinity	Few	1965
North Ormsby	Tees	Hospital Chapel	Board	1964
North Rigton	Yorks.N	St.John	Few	1961
North Shields	Tyne	Ch	Lectern	1938
North Shields	Tyne	Regent Fish Resturant	Dolly,Miniature	1958
North Shields	Tyne	St.Columba	Several	1955
North Shields	Tyne	St.Peter	Few	1938
North Wingfield	Derby	St.Lawrence	Few	1963
Northallerton	Yorks.N	All Saints	Large	1931
Northallerton	Yorks.N	Boys Co.Mod.School	Shield	1965
Northallerton	Yorks.N	Ch	Table	1954
Northallerton	Yorks.N	Ch	Prayer Desk	1958
Northallerton	Yorks.N	Choral Society	Stand	1968
Northallerton	Yorks.N	Friarage Hospital	Chairs	1955
Northallerton	Yorks.N	Methodist Ch	Lectern	1971
Northallerton	Yorks.N	NR Training College	Several	1949
Northallerton	Yorks.N	Police HQ	Trophy	1951
Northallerton	Yorks.N	Town Council	Case	1998
Northallerton	Yorks.N	Young Farmers	Shield	1970
Northallerton	Yorks.N	School	Shield	1946
Northenden	Lancs	St.Wilfrid	Large	1953
Northwich	Ches	Ch	Lectern	1966
Norton, Malton	Yorks.N	Rural Dist.Counc.	Board	1961
Norton, Malton	Yorks.N	St.Peter	Several	1937
Norton, Malton	Yorks.N	St.Mary	Few	1963
Norton on Tees	Tees	Ch	Lectern	1982
Norton on Tees	Tees	Methodist Ch	Seating	1963
Norton on Tees	Tees	Red House School	Few	1969
Norton on Tees	Tees	St.Mary	Several	1948
Norton on Tees	Tees	St.Michael	Few	1934
Norton on Tees	Tees	Wm.Newton Sec.Mod.Sch.	Platform Set	1957
Norwich	Norfolk	Holy Cross Stoke	Stand	1952
Norwich	Norfolk	RAF Horsham	Chair	1954
Nossmayo	Devon	Parish	Pews	
Nottingham	Notts	Bluecoat School	Several	1965
Nottingham	Notts	St.Barnabas RC Cathedral	Few	1933
Nottingham	Notts	St.Peter	Few	1950
Nottingham	Notts	Windley Baptist Chapel	Table	2003
Nuku'alofa	Tonga	Parliament Buildings	Chair	1993
Nunburnholme	Yorks.E	St.James	Altar rails	1946
Nunnington	Yorks.N	All Saints & St.James	Several	1929
Nunthorpe	Tees	Methodist Ch	Large	1960
Nunthorpe	Tees	St.Mary	Large	1940
Oakdale,Sheffield	Yorks.S	Oakdale School	Several	1954
Oakengates	Shrop	Priors Lee Hall	Few	1962
Oakham	Rutland	Oakham School	Several	1955
Old Byland	Yorks.N	Ch	Bench	1936
Old Byland	Yorks.N	The Green	Seat	1937
Old Swinford	Warks	St.Mary	Gates	1929
Oldham	Lancs	Counthill School	Missal stand	1997
Oldstead	Yorks.N	Black Swan Inn	Several	1930
Oldwinsford	Staffs	St.Mary	Gates	1929
Ollerton	Notts	Ollerton Hall	Several	1929
Ontario	Canada	Cayuga St.John	Candlestick	1996
Ormesby	Tees	Methodist Ch	Few	1957
Osmondthorpe	Yorks.W	St.Philip	Several	1930
Osmotherley	Yorks.N	St.Peter	Several	1939
Ossett	Yorks.W	Ch	Few	1947
Oswaldkirk	Yorks.N	St.Oswald	Stall	1947
Otley	Yorks.W	All Saints	Several	1950
Otley	Yorks.W	Council Chamber	Several	1951
Otteringham	Yorks.E	Ch	Board	1957
Otterington S	Yorks.N	St.Andrew	Several	1920
Otterington S.	Yorks.N	Institute	Fireplace	1954
Oulston	Yorks.N	Chapel	CredTable	1951
Outwood	Yorks.W	Ch	Few	1951
Owlston	Yorks.W	Ch	Reredos	1937
Owston,Sheffield	Yorks.S	All Saints	Several	1937
Oxford	Oxon	Crown and Thistle	Tables	1938
Oxford	Oxon	University College	Few	1998
Padiham	Lancs	St.Leonards	Few	1999
Pannal	Yorks.W	National Childrens' Home	Altar rails	1961
Pannal	Yorks.W	St.Robert	Several	1936

Place	Area	Site	Description	Earliest Date
Patrick Brompton	Yorks.N	St.Patrick	Few	1953
Patterdale	Cumbria	St.Patrick	Staves	1920
Peacehaven	Sussex	Peacehaven Hotel	Several	1959
Penistone	Yorks.S	St.John t Baptist	Tray	1997
Penmaermawr	Wales	St.Seiriol Chapel	Several	1961
Penwortham	Lancs	St.Leonard	Few	1956
Perth	Scot.N	Ch	Candlestick	1994
Peterborough	Cambs	Cathedral	Few	1935
Peterhead, NB	Canada	St.Peter Episcopalean	Reredos	
Pickering	Yorks.N	Forest and Vale Hotel	Several	1950
Pickering	Yorks.N	Low Hall Hotel	Few	1947
Pickering	Yorks.N	Stape	Chair	1998
Pickhill	Yorks.N	Ch	Psalm Board	1950
Picton	Yorks.N	Ch	Font cover	1959
Piercebridge	Durham	The George Hotel	Several	1935
Pluscarden	Scot.N	Priory	Stalls	1962
Pocklington	Yorks.E	All Saints	Altar rails	1926
Pocklington	Yorks.E	St.Mary Presbyterian	Few	1957
Pontefract	Yorks.W	Ch	Missal stand	1966
Pontefract	Yorks.W	Young Farmers Club	Plaque	1956
Ponteland	NLand	St.Mary	MemSeat	1989
Pontepool	Wales	St.Albans Convent School	Several	1963
Pool-i-Wharfedale	Yorks.W	CofESchool	Plaque	1975
Pool-i-Wharfedale	Yorks.W	St.Wilfrid Methodist	Several	1937
Pool-i-Wharfedale	Yorks.W	Pool Village Hall	Boards	1958
Poppleton	Yorks.N	Nether Poppleton Ch	Several	1939
Porthcawl	Wales	British Steel	Table	1998
Portsmouth	Sussex	North End School	Lectern	1962
Port Talbot	Wales	St.Agnes Margam Rd Ch	Several	1958
Potten End,Hemel	Herts	Holy Trinity Ch	Several	1967
Poulton-le-Fylde	Lancs	Ch	Few	1965
Preston	Lancs	Catholic College	Tablet	1953
Preston	Lancs	Hutton Vicarage	Few	1958
Pudsey	Yorks.W	Ch	Lectern	1988
Pudsey	Yorks.W	Fulneck Moravian Ch	Several	2000
Pudsey	Yorks.W	Grammar School	Tablet	1949
Pudsey	Yorks.W	Pudsey Ch	Several	1960
Purley	Surrey	Downside School	Board	1961
Purston	Yorks.W	St.Thomas	Several	1955
Quarr	IOW	Quarr Abbey	Large	1952
Quarrington	Durham	Ch.	Several	1952
Rainham	Kent	St.Margaret	Organ Case	1953
Ramsgill	Yorks.N	St.Mary	Few	1947
Rastrick	Yorks.W	St.John-t-Divine	Several	1959
Ratcliffe	Leics	Ratcliffe College	Several	1937
Rawcliffe Bridge	Yorks.E	St.Philip	Altar rails	1957
Reculver	Kent	St.Mary	Organ Case	1955
Redcar	Yorks.N	Newcomen School	Lectern	1956
Redcar	Yorks.N	Sacred Heart	Few	
Redcar	Yorks.N	St.Peter	Few	1936
Redcar	Yorks.N	Town Hall	Chair	1939
Redmire	Yorks.N	Ch	Lectern	1947
Repton	Derby	School	Reredos	
Retford	Notts	Council	Seal	1966
Retford	Notts	Ranby House School	Large	1958
Richmond	Yorks.N	Green Howards HQ Mess	Large	1936
Richmond	Yorks.N	Kings Hotel and Cafe	Fireplace	1929
Richmond	Yorks.N	Richmond School	Library	1953
Richmond	Yorks.N	St.Mary	Large	1932
Ridge	Herts	Ch	Several	1955
Rievaulx	Yorks.N	Ch	Figures	1932
Ripon	Yorks.N	Cathedral	Several	1937
Ripon	Yorks.N	Ripon Grammar School	Lectern	1950
Ripon	Yorks.N	Ripon YMCA	Shield	1999
Ripon	Yorks.N	St.Margaret	Walnut Stalls	1934
Ripon	Yorks.N	St.Mary	Lectern	
Ripon	Yorks.N	Training College	Several	1934
Ripon	Yorks.N	Unicorn Hotel	Fireplace	1951
Ripponden	Yorks.W	St.Bartholomew	Font Cover	1980

Place	Area	Site	Description	Earliest Date
Rochdale	Lancs	Ch	Several	1965
Rochdale	Lancs	Whitworth Methodist Ch	Lectern	1968
Rochester	Kent	Bridge Chapel	Several	1937
Rodley	Yorks.W	Rodley	Prayer Desk	1958
Rogate	Sussex	Church house	Few	1995
Roker	Durham	Methodist Ch	Few	1955
Roker	Durham	St.Andrews	Font Cover	1965
Romaldkirk	Durham	St.Romald	Several	1937
Romford	Essex	St.Alban	Boards	2002
Rossington	Yorks.S	St.Michael	Board	1965
Rotherham	Yorks.S	Waddington Shop	Several	1958
Rothwell	Yorks.W	Holy Trinity	Several	1997
Roundhay	Yorks.W	Congregational Ch	Table	1957
Roundhay	Yorks.W	St.Andrew United Reform	Chairs	
Rowsley	Derby	St.Catherine	Board	
Royal Navy	Yorks.W	HMS Ark Royal Chapel	Chairs	1954
Royds Mount	Yorks.S	St.Davids Prep Sch	Several	1948
Ruswarp	Yorks.N	St.Bartholemew	Several	1920
Saddleworth	Yorks.S	Ch	Screen	1958
Saffron Walden	Essex	Ashdon Hall	Prayer Desk	1953
Saltburn	Yorks.N	County Infant School	Tablet	1969
Saltburn	Yorks.N	Inner Wheel	Wheel	1954
Saltley	Durham	Ch	Doors	1966
Sand Hutton	Yorks.N	St.Leonard	Few	1913
Sandal Magna	Yorks.S	St.Helen	Several	1963
Sandbach	Ches	St.Winifrid	Few	1968
Sanderstead	Surrey	Ch	Table	1961
Sandhurst	Berks	Royal Military Academy	Few	2002
Sandsend	Yorks.N	St.Mary	Altar rails	1956
Sandwich	Kent	Rectory	Several	1985
Saxton	Yorks.W	Ch	Several	1948
Scarborough	Yorks.N	College	Few	1965
Scarborough	Yorks.N	Cricket Club	Several	1950
Scarborough	Yorks.N	Harbour Masonic Lodge	Chair	
Scarborough	Yorks.N	Hospital Mortuary	Few	1964
Scarborough	Yorks.N	North Riding Training College	Few	1962
Scarborough	Yorks.N	Prince of Wales Hotel	Beds	1936
Scarborough	Yorks.N	Queen Margaret's School	Few	1938
Scarborough	Yorks.N	St.Columba	Several	1937
Scarborough	Yorks.N	St.Edward	Few	1995
Scarborough	Yorks.N	St.James	Large	
Scarborough	Yorks.N	St.Luke	Several	1932
Scarborough	Yorks.N	St.Martin	Few	1938
Scarborough	Yorks.N	St.Mary	Lectern	1983
Scarborough	Yorks.N	St.Saviour	Few	1954
Scarborough	Yorks.N	Woodlands Crematorium	Several	1960
Scarcroft	Yorks.W	Golf Club	Several	2002
Scarcroft	Yorks.W	Scarcroft Ch	Plaque	1996
Scarthingwell	Yorks W	Hall	Few	
Scawton	Yorks.N	Farmers Arms Inn	Stools	1971
Scawton	Yorks.N	St.Mary	Prayer Desk	1995
Scotstoun	Scot.C	Scotstoun Shipyard	Boards	1945
Scotton	Yorks.N	St.Thomas	Several	1959
Sculcoates	Yorks.E	St.Paul	Several	1934
Scunthorpe	Lincs	Sysaghts Steel Works	Boardroom	1956
Scunthorpe	Lincs	Techical High School	Chairs	1957
Scunthorpe	Lincs	Ch	Lectern	
Seaford	Sussex	St.Peter	Lectern	1947
Seaham	Durham	St.Mary	Altar	1964
Seaham	Durham	Masonic Temple	Chairs	1971
Seamer	Yorks.N	St.Martin	Few	1944
Seascale	Cumbria	Vicarage	Few	1987
Seaton	Cumbria	St.Paul	Few	1970
Seaton Carew	Durham	Holy Trinity	Several	1939
Seaton Carew	Durham	New Ridley Ch	CredTable,	1955
Sedbergh	Yorks.N	Sedbergh School	Tablet	1948
Sedgefield	Durham	Ch	Chair	2001
Sefton	Lancs	St.Helen	Few	1981
Seghill	NLand	Holy Trinity	Several	1994

Altar at Saxton church, near Tadcaster, with adzed panels and carved foliage that acts as ribbon banding. Completed in 1948.

Place	Area	Site	Description	Earliest Date
Selby	Yorks.E	Abbey	Few	1955
Selby	Yorks.E	Hambleton	Lectern	1999
Selby	Yorks.E	High School	Board	1958
Selby	Yorks.E	Salvation Army	CredTable	1987
Selby	Yorks.E	Stelling Hall	Lectern	1954
Sessay	Yorks.N	St.Cuthbert	Several	1951
Settrington	Yorks.N	All Saints	Large	1922
Sevenoaks	Kent	Esher College	Several	1986
Sewerby	Yorks.E	St.John	Board	1959
Shadforth	Durham	St.Cuthbert	Chair	1962
Shadwell	Yorks.W	Shadwell Ch	Several	1947
Sheerness	Kent	Sheppey Girls High Sch	Several	1964
Sheffield	Yorks.S	Ch	Table	1963
Sheffield	Yorks.S	Ch	Panelling	1960
Sheffield	Yorks.S	Fulwood Ch	Stall	1958
Sheffield	Yorks.S	High Storrs School	Lectern	1962
Sheffield	Yorks.S	Moorwood Ltd.	Boardroom	1959
Sheffield	Yorks.S	Meadowhead Presbytery	Candlesticks	1999
Sheffield	Yorks.S	Sheffield Twistdrill & Steel Co.	Boardroom	1964
Sheffield	Yorks.S	Upper Chapel	Chairs	1969
Shelf	Yorks.W	St.Michael & All Angels	Bench	1982
Sherbourne	Dorset	Sherbourne Prep. School	Furniture	
Sherburn	Durham	Christs Hospital	Plaque	1999
Sherburn-in-Elmet	Yorks.W	Red Bear Inn	Several	1963
Shifnal	Shrop	Ch	Pascal stick	1985
Shildon	Durham	St.John	Several	1962
Shipley	Yorks.W	Browgate Vicarage	Candlestick	1995
Shipley	Yorks.W	Salt High School	Tablet	1950
Shipley	Yorks.W	St.Peter	Plates	1962
Shipton-on-Ouse	Yorks.N	Holy Evangelist	Gates	1968
Shirley	Hants	Roman Catholic Ch	Doors	
Shirley	Warks	Shermans Cross GHSchool	Missal stand	1962
Shirley	Warks	TSB College,Monkspath	Lectern	
Shotley Bridge	Durham	St.Cuthbert	CredTable	1937
Shrewsbury	Shrop	Oldhams Hall	Chairs	1961
Sicklinghall	Yorks.W	Immaculate Conception Ch	Large	1941
Siddal, Halifax	Yorks.W	St.Mark	Altar rails	1963
Simonsbath	Somset	Exmoor Vicarage	Board	1962
Sinnington	Yorks.N	All Saints	Altar	1955
Skipsea	Yorks.E	All Saints	Lectern	1954
Skipton	Yorks.N	Castle	Large	1971
Skipton	Yorks.N	Christchurch	Several	1948
Skipton	Yorks.N	Council Chamber	Large	1960
Skipton	Yorks.N	Holy Trinity	Bookcase	1956
Skipton-on-Swale	Yorks.N	RCAF Station	Bar	1944
Skipton-on-Swale	Yorks.N	Skipton Bridge Ch	Chair	1945
Skipwith	Yorks.E	St.Helen	Several	1964
Slaithwaite	Yorks.W	Holy Family Ch	Pascal stick	2003
Sledmere	Yorks.E	St.Mary	Mem.Case	1951
Slingsby	Yorks.N	All Saints	Few	1947
Slough	Bucks	Horlicks	Boardroom	1925
Slough	Bucks	ICI Paints Div.	Large	1940
Smethwick	Staffs	Council chamber	Boards	1968
Snainton	Yorks.N	St.Stephen	Few	1936
Snaith	Yorks.S	Holy Trinity	Few	1962
Snape	Yorks.N	Methodist Ch	Several	1958
Solihull	Warks	Borough Council	Boards	1967
South Cave	Yorks.E	All Saints	Cross	1944
South Elmsall	Yorks.S	St.Mary	Reredos	1949
South Hylton	Durham	Ch	Lectern	1995
South Kirkby	Yorks.W	All Saints	Several	1941
South Milford	Yorks.W	St.Mary	Large	1954
South Moor	Durham	St.George	Large	1937
South Otterington	Yorks.N	Ch	Few	1920
South Shields	Tyne	All Saints	Prayer Desk	1982
South Shields	Tyne	Seamans Mission Chapel	Tryptych	1953
South Shields	Tyne	St.Hilda	Few	1948
South Stainley	Yorks.N	Ch	Altar	1944
South Westoe	Tyne	St.Michael & All Angels	Prayer Desk	1982

Place	Area	Site	Description	Earliest Date
Southam	Warks	St.James	Prayer Desk	2000
Southampton	Hants	East Wessex TAVR HQ	Plaque	1981
Southport	Lancs	King George V School	Tablets	1948
Southport	Lancs	Soroptimists Club	Missal stand	1970
Southwell	Notts	Minster	Large	1949
Southwold	Suffolk	St.Edmund K & Martyr	Few	1969
Sowerby	Yorks.N	Methodist Ch	Few	1962
Sowerby	Yorks.N	St.Oswald	Few	1956
Sowerby Bridge	Yorks.W	Christchurch	Several	1965
Spalding	Lincs	St.John	Large	1938
Spalding	Lincs	St.Mary Mission Hall Weston	Pulpit	
Spennithorpe	Yorks.N	Ch	Few	1947
Spennymoor	Durham	Council Chamber	Few	1961
Spennymoor	Durham	St.Andrew	Kneelers	1953
Spofforth	Yorks.W	All Saints	Several	1952
Sponden	Derby	St.Werburgh	Lectern	1962
Sproxton	Yorks.N	St.Chad	Stool	1997
St.Albans	Herts	United Reform	Font	1955
St.Austell	Cornwall	Vicarage	Prayer Desks	1963
St.Davids	Wales	Cathedral	Large	1955
St.Helens	Lancs	Notre Dame School	Few	1957
St.Helens	Lancs	St.Helen	Few	1957
St.Helens	Lancs	St.Thomas	Several	1961
St.Helier	CI	Royal Yacht Hotel	Medium	1969
St.Johns Wood	Bucks	All Saints	Few	1939
St.Peter Port	CI	Ch	Few	1997
Staincross	Yorks.W	Ch	Few	1964
Staindrop	Durham	Deanery	Few	1965
Stainton	Tees	St.Peter & Paul	Several	1956
Staintondale	Yorks.N	Chapel	Lectern	2001
Stanbrook	Worcs	Abbey of St.Mary	Very large	1926
Standish Wigan	Lancs	Notre Dame Convent	Seating	1964
Standish	Glos	St.Nicholas	Few	1922
Stanley	Durham	Blue Bell Inn	Several	1963
Stanley	Durham	Ch	CredTable	1933
Stanningley	Yorks.W	St.Thomas	Few	1964
Stape	Yorks.N	Ch	Chair	1998
Starbeck	Yorks.N	St.Andrew Methodist Ch	Few	1960
Startforth	Durham	Ch	Candlesticks	1956
Staverton	Somset	St.Paul de Lyon	Altar	
Stevenage	Herts	St.Nicholas Old Ch	Seating	1963
Stewartby	Beds	United Reform Ch	Tablet	1970
Stillingfleet	Yorks.N	St.Helen	Few	1976
Stillington	Yorks.N	St.Nicholas	Several	1935
Stillington	Yorks.N	W I Hall	Banner Pole	
Stockton on Tees	Tees	Blakeston Community Sch.	Lectern	2002
Stockton on Tees	Tees	Congregational Ch	Font	1967
Stockton on Tees	Tees	Grammar School	Lectern	1956
Stockton on Tees	Tees	Holy Trinity	Several	1935
Stockton on Tees	Tees	Holy TrinityCE School	Plaque	1968
Stockton on Tees	Tees	St.Cuthbert	Chairs	1960
Stockton on Tees	Tees	St.Mary RC	Furnishings	1976
Stockton on Tees	Tees	St.Paul	Few	
Stockton	Wilts	Green Howards Ch	Mem.Chair	1970
Stockton-on-Forest	Yorks.N	Holy Trinity	Several	1923
Stockton-on-Forest	Yorks.N	Village Hall	Tablet	1966
Stoke Poges	Bucks	Duffield House	Few	1985
Stokesley	Yorks.N	St.Peter & Paul	Several	1939
Stokesley	Yorks.N	Town Hall	Doors	1967
Stone	Staffs	Ch	Prayer Desks	1970
Stonegrave	Yorks.N	Holy Trinity	Few	1941
Stoney Stanton	Leics	St.Michael	Several	1963
Stranton	Durham	Stranton Ch	Few	1965
Stratford-o-Avon	Warks	Austin Reed's Shop	Several	
Streat	Sussex	Woodard School	Lectern	1954
Strensall	Yorks.N	St. Mary	Several	1948
Stutton,Tadcaster	Yorks.W	Stutton Ch	Font	1964
Summerbridge	Durham	Council Chamber	Few	1960
Sunderland	Durham	Ch	Stand	1996

Western screen war memorial at South Kirkby church, near Pontefract, with the adzing especially prominent.

Exquisite choir frontal at Southwell Minster, Nottinghamshire, which would have taken many weeks to complete. The order was placed in 1949.

Place	Area	Site	Description	Earliest Date
Sunderland	Durham	All Saints	Cupboard	1965
Sunderland	Durham	Bonnersfield Restaurant	Few	1968
Sunderland	Durham	Christchurch	Font	1968
Sunderland	Durham	Holy Rosary/Imm.Heart Pres.	Several	1999
Sunderland	Durham	Methodist Ch	Few	1955
Sunderland	Durham	NFU Board Room	Few	1951
Sunderland	Durham	Rowe Hotel	Few	1982
Sunderland	Durham	St.Nicholas	Lectern	1977
Sunderland	Durham	Sunderland Water Co.	Chairs	1970
Sutton	Yorks.N	Ch	Several	1970
Sutton Coldfield	Warks	Ch	Few	1970
Sutton-on- Hull	Yorks.E	St.James	Several	1969
Sutton Valence	Kent	Ch	Boards	1960
Sutton-on-Derwent	Yorks.E	St.Micheal & All Angels	Few	1928
Sutton-on-Forest	Yorks.N	All Souls	Several	1922
Sutton-on-Trent	Notts	Ch.	Crucifix	1927
Sutton-u-WSC	Yorks.N	Sutton Hall	Mem.Tablet	1949
Swarcliffe	Yorks.N	Baptist Ch.	Few	1960
Swillington	Yorks.W	Ch	Cross	1921
Tadcaster	Yorks.W	John Smiths Brewery	Tables	1961
Tadcaster	Yorks.W	Peace Centre	Several	1996
Tadcaster	Yorks.W	RAF Kirkby Wharf	Few	1941
Tadcaster	Yorks.W	Rotary Club	Wheel	1958
Tadcaster	Yorks.W	St.Mary	Chairs	2003
Tain,Invergordon	Scot.N	St.Andrew	Several	1935
Tamworth	Leics	St.Joseph's Convent	Several	1932
Tan Hill	Yorks.N	Tan Hill Inn	Furniture	1946
Tanfield	Yorks.N	Cricket Club	Plaque	1958
Tanfield	Yorks.N	St.Nicholas	Several	1937
Taplow	Bucks	Burnham Abbey	Few	1957
Tarleton	Lancs	Holy Trinity	Few	1962
Tealby	Lincs	All Saints	Few	1944
Temple Sowerby	Cumbria	Hall	Doors	1935
Terrington	Yorks.N	All Saints	Seat	1951
Thaxted	Essex	St.John the Baptist	Various	
Thirkleby	Yorks.N	All Saints	Several	1928
Thirsk	Yorks.N	Franciscan Priory	Several	1956
Thirsk	Yorks.N	Golden Fleece Hotel	Several	1961
Thirsk	Yorks.N	RAF	Trophy	1948
Thirsk	Yorks.N	Council Offices	Board	1974
Thirsk	Yorks.N	Rotary Club	Few	1938
Thirsk	Yorks.N	Secondary School	Boards	1957
Thirsk	Yorks.N	St.Mary	Several	1920
Thirsk	Yorks.N	Thirsk Hall	Tablet	1960
Thornaby	Tees	Private Chapel	Several	1956
Thornaby	Tees	St.Paul	Several	1937
Thornbury	Yorks.W	Thornbury Ch	Board	1963
Thornley	Durham	Ch	Few	1961
Thornthwaite	Cumbria	Blessed Virgin Mary	Chair	1969
Thornton Watlass	Yorks.N	St.Mary the Virgin	Several	1953
Thornton Watless	Yorks.N	Chapel at Hall	Few	1933
Thornton-le-Dale	Yorks.N	All Saints	Several	1945
Thornton-le-Moor	Yorks.N	All Saints	Few	1954
Thorp Arch	Yorks.W	All Saints	Large	1932
Thorpe Bay	Essex	Ch	Few	2000
Thorpe Thewles	Tees	Ch	Few	1967
Thorpe Thewles	Tees	St.James Grindon	Case	1995
Thurlstone	Yorks.S	St.Saviour	Prayer Desk	1971
Ticehurst	Sussex	St.Mary	Several	1961
Tideswell	Derby	St.John the Baptist	Few	
Todmorden	Lancs	Grammar School	Few	1965
Topcliffe	Yorks.N	Q.Mary's Sch.(Dunc.Park)	Collection	1937
Topcliffe	Yorks.N	Skellfield School	Tablet	1968
Topcliffe	Yorks.N	St.John	Tablets	1970
Troon	Scot.S	St.Ninian	Few	1936
Tunstall	Yorks.E	All Saints	Cred.Table	1964
Tynemouth	NLand	St.Augustin	Choir Stalls	early
Undy,Gwent	Wales	St.Mary	Bookcase	1996
Upminster	Essex	St.Laurence	Seating	1954
Uppingham	Rutland	Uppingham School	Large	1950
Upsall	Yorks.N	Upsall Castle	Staircase	1924
Upton	Devon	Ch	Missal stand	1957
Upton	Yorks.W	Ch	Altar rails	1954
Usk	Wales	Ch	Gates	1965
Utley	Yorks.W	St.Mark	Chair	1969
Uttoxeter	Staffs	Denston College	Large	1957
Virden,Manitoba	Canada	Virden Clinic	Several	1962
Virginia Water	Surrey	Few		1987
Wainfleet	Lancs	All Saints	Altar rails	1956
Wakefield	Yorks.W	Cathedral	Large	1940
Wakefield	Yorks.W	Ch Market St	MemTablet	1953
Wakefield	Yorks.W	Crofton	Chair	1997
Wakefield	Yorks.W	Girls High School	Several	1936
Wakefield	Yorks.W	Pinderfields Hospital Chapel	Several	1962
Wakefield	Yorks.W	St.Johns Primary School	Lectern	1968
Wakefield	Yorks.W	Stanley Royd Hospital	Several	1960
Waltham	Lincs	All Saints	Few	1962
Walton	Oxon	St.Peter	Several	1967
Ware	Herts	St.Edmunds College	Table	1966
Ware	Herts	Ch	Prayer Desk	1953
Wareham	Dorset	Bovington Camp RAC HQ	Chairs	1981
Warehorne	Kent	St.Mathew	Stands	1965
Wargrave	Berks	St.Mary	CredTable	1967
Warminster	Wilts	Royal Welsh 1stBat.	Table	1989
Warrick Bridge	Cumbria	Ch	Altar rails	1948
Warrington	Lancs	Paddington House Hotel	Trolleys	1971
Warrington	Lancs	S.Lancs.Reg.Chapel	Few	1968
Warton	Lancs	St.Oswald	Chairs	1969
Washington	Durham	Training College	Lectern	
Washington DC	USA	Ch	Missal stand	1983
Wass	Yorks.N	St.Thomas Mission Chapel	Several	1937
Waterloo	Yorks.W	St.Mary	Several	1935
Watford	Herts	Reeds School	Library	1940
Waukegan,Illinois	USA	St.Paul Lutheran Ch	Several	2005
Wednesbury	Staffs	St.Francis	Seating	1964
Well	Yorks.N	Ch	Several	1935
Well	Yorks.N	Well Hall	Fireplaces	1931
Wells	Somset	Cathedral	Several	1958
Wembley	Midsex	Oil & Colour Chem.Assoc	Chair	1987
Wensley	Yorks.N	Holy Trinity	Several	1941
West Ayton	Yorks.N	Methodist Ch	Altar	1960
West Butterwick	Lincs	Meths.Ch	Font	1969
West Linton	Scot.S	Blyth Bridge	Few	1995
West Rounton	Yorks.N	St.Oswald	Lectern	1969
West Tanfield	Yorks.N	Bruce Arms	Stools	1969
West Tanfield	Yorks.N	St.Nicholas	Several	1934
West Witton	Yorks.N	St.Bartholomew	Several	1961
Weston	Yorks.W	All Saints	Doors	1972
Weston-on-Trent	Derby	St.Andrews	Altar rails	
Westow	Yorks.E	St.Mary	Pulpit	1951
Wetherby	Yorks.W	St.James RC	Several	1958
Weybridge	Surrey	Ch	Table	1939
Wheatley	Yorks.S	Ch	Prayer Desk	1967
Wheldrake	York	St.Helen	Few	1958
Whenby	Yorks.N	Ch	Pulpit	1922
Whitby	Yorks.N	Rowing Club	Chair	1969
Whitby	Yorks.N	St. Hildas School	Large	1934
Whitby	Yorks.N	St.Hilda's Priory	Large	1934
Whitby	Ches	St.Thomas	Few	1995
Whitehaven	Cumbria	Whitehaven G School	Few	1962
Whitely	Wilts	Ch	Reredos	1935
Whitkirk	Yorks.W	Ch	Few	1961
Whitley Bay	NLand	Victoria Hotel	Settle	1936
Whitley Bay	NLand	Ch	Chair	1966
Whittington	Staffs	Officers Mess	Tables	1938
Wickwar	Glos	Holy Trinity	Stall	1930
Wigan	Lancs	Clubhouse	Board	1962
Wigan	Lancs	Forster Ltd, Haigh	Office	1996

Place	Area	Site	Description	Earliest Date
Wiggington	York	St.Mary	Lectern	1982
Wilberfoss	Yorks.E	St.John the Baptist	Few	1964
Wincanton	Somset	Stavordale Priory	Furniture	1967
Winchester	Hants	Cathedral	Kneelers	1933
Windermere	Cumbria	St.Mary	Board	1955
Wingate	Durham	Ch	Candlesticks	1944
Winkburn	Notts	St.John of Jerusalem	Few	1935
Winksley	Yorks.N	St.Cuthbert	Prayer Desk	1937
Winsford	Ches	Verdin Grammar School	Lectern	
Wisbech	Cambs	St.Mary	Few	1938
Wistow	Yorks.E	All Saints	Few	1982
Wistow	Yorks.N	All Saints	Several	1936
Wistow	Cambs	Ch	Few	1936
Withington	Glos	The Mill Inn	Several	
Witton Park	Durham	Ch	Board	1966
Woking	Surrey	Golf Club	Furniture	1992
Wollaton	Notts	St.Leonard	Few	1971
Wolverhampton	Staffs	Girls High School	Platform Set	1971
Wolviston	Durham	Chapel	Altar	1954
Womersley	Yorks.S	Womersley Ch	Gravecross	1966
Woodborough	Notts	Ch	Lectern	1967
Woodhall	Yorks.N	School	Few	1940
Woodkirk	Yorks.W	St.Mary	Prayer Desk	1954
Woodlesford	Yorks.W	All Saints	Several	1948
Woolley	Somset	All Saints	Few	1966
Woolley	Yorks.W	St.Peter	Few	1966
Wootton Glanville	Dorset	Ch	Several	1957
Wordlesdon	Surrey	Insurance Hall	Missal stand	1998
Workington	Cumbria	Our Lady Priory	Large	1921
Workington	Cumbria	St.John	Candlesticks	1969
Worksop	Notts	Boldry Ltd	Few	1956
Worksop	Notts	St.Anne	Altar rails	1948
Worksop	Notts	St.Mary	Doors	
Worksop	Notts	Waddington's Shop	Several	1958
Worksop	Notts	Worksop College	Several	1956
Worsborough	Yorks.S	St.Mary	Few	1986
Worthen	Shrop	All Saints	Prayer Desk	1951
Wortley	Yorks.W	St.John	Several	1949
Wortley	Yorks.W	Wortley Village Hall	Few	1968
Worton	Lancs	St.Joseph Home	Seating	1966
Wotton	Somset	Tytherington Ch	Few	1996
Wragby	Yorks.W	Ch	Prayer Desk	1969
Wrangthorn	Yorks.W	St.Augustine	Cross	1950
Wrexham	Wales	Maelor Hospital Chapel	Several	1966
Wycliffe	Durham	St.Mary	Several	1948
Wykeham	Yorks.N	St.Helen & All Saints	Several	1935
Wythenshawe	Lancs	St.Peter	Pulpit	1962
Yarm	Tees	Grammar School	Lectern	1948
Yarm	Tees	St.Mary Mag.	Altar rails	1948
Yeadon	Yorks.W	Aireborough School	Tablet	1949
Yearsley	Yorks.N	Parish Ch	Pulpit	1909
Yeovil	Somset	St.John the Baptist	Several	1961
York	York	Abbey Park Hotel	Tables	1967
York	York	All Saints Pavement	Several	1931
York	York	Bar Convent	Statue	1958
York	York	Beckfield Lane School	Lectern	1952
York	York	Ben Johnson Printers	Boardroom	1982
York	York	British Legion Melrosegate	Several	1956
York	York	City Library	Seats	1946
York	York	College for Girls	Table	1938
York	York	Convent Poor Clares	Crucifix	1954
York	York	Guildhall	Several	1944
York	York	Hospital	Carving	1938
York	York	Medical Society	Few	1933
York	York	Melbourne Terr. Meth.Ch	Few	1959
York	York	Merchant Adventurers Hall	Chair	1940
York	York	Mill Mount School	Platform Set	1935
York	York	Minster	Very large	1935
York	York	NFU	Few	1997
York	York	NR Mental Hospital	Few	1948
York	York	Purey Cust Chapel	Tablet	1933
York	York	Queen Annes Grammar Sch	Several	1950
York	York	Royal Signals Mess	Bar	1996
York	York	South Bank Ch	Few	1954
York	York	St.Chad	Several	1926
York	York	St.Clement	Large	1924
York	York	St.Johns College	Large	1911
York	York	St.Lawrence	Several	1932
York	York	St.Luke	Few	1941
York	York	St.Martin	Few	1938
York	York	St.Mary Bishophill	Altar	1930
York	York	St.Maurice	Figure	1923
York	York	St.Michael-le-Belfry	Lectern	1943
York	York	St.Olave	Several	1936
York	York	St.Olave School	Board	
York	York	St.Paul	Board	1958
York	York	St.Peter's School	Several	1929
York	York	St.Philip & James	Altar	
York	York	St.Stephen Orphanage	Tablet	1938
York	York	St.Thomas	Several	1943
York	York	St.Williams College	Doors	1935
York	York	Terry & Co	Trophy	1949
York	York	The Retreat	Chair	1938
York	York	Youth Hostel	Fireplace	1940

HANNAH HAUXWELL
80 Years in the Dales
By W R Mitchell
The Official Biography to Celebrate the 80th Birthday of this Remarkable Dales Character
Thirty-five years ago, Hannah Hauxwell captured the hearts of the nation when she was the subject of an extraordinary television documentary, Too Long a Winter, which portrayed her constant struggle on a remote Pennine farm with no electricity and no running water.

The TV programme made her a national celebrity and a further fifteen television programmes followed. She went on memorable tours of Europe and America, shook hands with the Pope and played the piano on the Orient Express.

Now, in her 80th year, Hannah lives alone but content in a Teesdale village. This major book, by the renowned writer on the dales, W R Mitchell, traces the extraordinary life of a delightful personality who has never lost her links with the dales countryside. It includes many previously unpublished photographs.
Fully illustrated. Hardback.

ESSENCE OF THE YORKSHIRE COAST
By Malcolm Barker
A beautifully illustrated book, featuring recently discovered archive photography.
This book goes behind the scenery to look in depth at life and work along the coast. It puts a new perspective on such subjects as fishing, smuggling, shipping and shipwrecks, and the proud story of lifeboats putting to sea in conditions of dire peril. It focuses on communities large and small, ranging from trawling out of Hull to the traditional fishing village of Staithes, and from Scarborough in its heyday to life at remote Spurn Point.
Fully illustrated. Hardback.

ESSENCE OF WHITBY
By Malcolm Barker
A superbly researched and beautifully illustrated book that looks in depth at the history of this popular seaside town. Glorious photographs enhance Malcolm Barker's illuminating, informative text.
Fully illustrated. Hardback.

YORKSHIRE IN PARTICULAR
An Alternative A-Z
Edited by Michael Hickling
Foreword by Gervase Phinn
Asked to 'spell out' the essence of Yorkshire, journalists on the county's leading newspaper, The Yorkshire Post, have gathered together a diverse selection of people, places, products and peculiarities. The result is a book that will be treasured by all who have a special affection for this fascinating region.
Fully illustrated. Hardback.

A YEAR OF FAMILY RECIPES
by Lesley Wild
Customers at Bettys and Bettys Cookery School have been asking for a cookery book for years. A Year of Family Recipes is a personal collection of over 100 recipes by Lesley Wild from the Bettys family.
This 260 page hardbacked book covers everything from bread and jam making to suppers and salads; home baking and sophisticated entertaining.
Stunning photographs. Hardback.

Visit www.greatnorthernbooks.co.uk